15863
R795

The story of the RAC International Rally

The story of the RAC International Rally

Phil Drackett

ISBN 0 85429 270 5

First published under the title 'Rally of the Forests' by Pelham Books Ltd in 1970. This revised and enlarged edition published September 1980.

A FOULIS Motoring book

Printed in England by the publishers
Haynes Publishing Group
Sparkford, Yeovil, Somerset BA22 7JJ, England

Distributed in North America by
Haynes Publications Inc
861 Lawrence Drive, Newbury Park, California 91320, USA

Editor: **Jeff Clew**
Cover design: **Phill Jennings**
Layout design: **Rowland Smith**

Publishers Note:
Very few photographs of the pre-war and early post-war RAC Rallies exist and in consequence some of the photographs used in the early Chapters of this book may appear to be out of sequence. They have, however, been selected by the Author because some common thread exists that will link these photographs with the text.

Contents

**To
Jack Kemsley**

"My style is a lot of going sideways"
Hannu Mikkola

The Curtain Comes Down

NOT MANY novels and even fewer TV movies have happy endings these days. So it was a bit of a surprise when the 1979 Lombard-RAC International Rally of Great Britain ended very much in the fashion many people hoped for — an eighth successive victory for the most remarkable rally car of all time, the Ford Escort.

True it was not quite according to the script which should have provided a third win for veteran British driver Roger Clark instead of two on the trot for the equally-experienced Finn, Hannu Mikkola, but it was near enough to make Ford's Stuart Turner and Peter Ashcroft and a million or two rally enthusiasts feel that Henry was in his Heaven and all was right with the rally world.

Why such a weight of sentiment in a notoriously unsentimental sport?

In brief and before the 1979 event commenced, Ford had announced that, win or lose, this was to be a farewell appearance for the works team. Ford were to take a two years Sabbatical and use the time for research and development into the type of car needed to win rallies in the eighties.

Following a policy of moving around the country, the ancient Roman fortress of Chester on the Welsh border was chosen as the start and finish point of the 1979 Rally and crowds lined the historic streets as far as the eye could see when the cars set off from outside the Grosvenor Hotel on a chill but clear and sunny Sunday morning.

Hannu Mikkola, as winner in 1978, bore Number One and was flagged away by His Grace The Duke of Westminster who, apart from being one of London's biggest landlords, also owns sizeable chunks of Chester, including the Grosvenor.

9

THE STORY OF THE RAC INTERNATIONAL RALLY

The rally had been cut down by organiser Jim Porter from five days to four thus saving on petrol, hotel bills and expenses generally. The mileage was thus reduced to 1,700 but the tough part was much the same — some 450 miles of special stages, most of them through the forests, although for the first day, "Stately Home stages" predominated in order to give spectators the maximum chance of seeing the cars in action.

The field was limited to 175 starters but, in fact, well over 200 cars from 19 nations had entered. They came from Australia, Belgium, West Germany, East Germany, Denmark, France, Greece, Italy, Ireland, Japan, Norway, New Zealand, Sweden, Finland, the Soviet Union, Turkey, USA and South Africa.

Most of the great teams which had implanted their name on the rally in modern times were there to contest the last round of the World Championship — Saab, Nissan-Datsun, Lancia, Skoda, Wartburg, Polski-Fiat, Toyota, Audi, BL Cars, Dealer Team Vauxhall, Dealer Opel Team and, of course, the Fords. And there was also an official Russian Lada team.

The list of drivers too read like a roll call of the great. From Finland came Mikkola, Alen, Vatanen, Airikkala, Salonen and Lampinen; from Sweden Waldegard, Stig Blomqvist, Eklund, Danielson and Stromberg. West Germany contributed champion Walter Rohrl and Australia their champion, Greg Carr.

And the British contingent was the strongest for many a year. Headed by Roger Clark, it included the man most see as his natural successor, Russell Brookes, Tony Pond driving the new Talbot Sunbeam Lotus, John Taylor, British National Champion Malcolm Wilson, Jimmy McRae, Andy Dawson, Graham Elsmore and Brian Culcheth.

That French hero of many an RAC struggle, Jean-Luc Therier, was back but driving a Japanese Toyota. And there was interest too in the newest discovery amongst the girls — a little blonde wearing big Laplander boots and with the almost unpronounceable name of Geunda Eadie.

But however many times one surveyed the entry list, the odds on a Ford victory seemed ever more certain. Few manufacturers could ever have fielded a team of drivers like Mikkola, Waldegard, Vatanen, Clark and Brookes. There simply had to be a winner amongst them.

And so it proved.

But not before some excitement provided by Tony Pond, the driver who had made some spectacular attempts during the past season or two to put British Leyland back on the motor sport map. Now his fiery combative spirit had been allied to another manufacturer in distress, Chrysler. And he was

Start of the 1979 RAC in the historic city of Chester

Roger Clark, top Briton

Hannu Mikkola, winner of the 1978 and 1979 rallies

Peter Ashcroft, Ford's Competitions Manager

Stuart Turner, master strategist

Jim Porter, present-day organiser of the RAC Rally

Markku Alen, Finland....

Ari Vatanen, Finland....

driving a car on which the company pinned great hopes — a Lotus-powered version of the little Sunbeam, now being marketed under the new/old family name of Talbot.

The little car went like a bomb and as the cars went through Wales on the last night, Pond against all the odds was in third place. It was a night of freezing fog and black ice and on an ice covered bridge, Pond lost it, spun off and crashed into the ditch below. Even then, all might not have been lost but before he could even begin to struggle back on the road, a following car also skidded off the bridge and landed on top of the little Talbot. So the gallant newcomer which had done so well on its debut met an inglorious end. 'I'm simply too sick to say a word about it,' said Pond, 'we were going like a dream.'

For Finland's Markku Alen that treacherous night in Mid-Wales brought surprisingly better fortune. After a good start he had lost ground through some of the mechanical ills which affected his beautiful but temperamental Lancia Stratos. Now through the fog and the ice he stormed over the special stages as if they were bone-dry race circuits and clawed his way back into contention.

But oblivious to it all, Mikkola surged steadily on through that night and the next day and as the crowds waited in the darkness of cobbled Castle Square, it was the blue and white Escort which gently rolled forward to the fanfare of trumpets reserved for the winner.

There wasn't a scratch on the £20,000 car and mechanic Mick Jones said, 'Nothing went wrong with the car at all. He didn't even get a puncture.'

Yet Mikkola had been fastest man on 24 of the 59 stages and had finished with more than a ten-minute margin over his British team-mate. Russell Brookes, driving as usual under the sponsorship of Andrews Heat For Hire — which doesn't seem an inappropriate name.

Timo Salonen, with the experienced British co-driver Stuart Pegg sitting beside him, brought his Datsun into third place, thus preventing a Ford 1-2-3.

Vatanen, who looked likely to be second for most of the rally, took his Escort into a time control too early and the consequent penalty dropped him down to fourth place. Alen's fireworks display on the last night earned fifth place for his Stratos and veteran British driver John Taylor brought his Escort in sixth.

Just as pleased were Dealer Team Vauxhall because Finland's Pentti Airikkala, driving steadily, finished seventh and by so doing took the British Open Championship. He had won three international rallies during the

One of the Eaton's Yale-sponsored Fords takes to the water....

15

Simo   Lampinen, Finland....

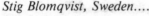

Per Eklund, Sweden....

Stig Blomqvist, Sweden....

Walter Rohrl, West Germany....

'An Awfully Big Adventure'

AN AWFULLY big adventure. That was the lure dreamed up for the Second RAC Rally by the versatile, publicity-conscious mind of Captain Phillips. Of the sucess of the 1932 event there could be no doubt and arrangements were soon in hand for 1933. Hastings was chosen as the finish this time and the dates March 14th to 18th.

The 'big adventure' was the prospect of spending two days and two nights continuously on the road, a prospect attractive enough to bring in no less than 357 entries.

Most of the big names were back again and some more to boot. There was Mrs 'Bill' Wisdom, versed in the art of hurtling a racing car around the Weybridge circuit faster than most men; Sammy Davis, winner of that extraordinary Le Mans after the pile-up at White House; woman speedway rider Fay Taylour; two more outstanding racing girls, Joan Richmond and Kay Petre; and two men known in other fields, F. Gordon Crosby, the famed *Autocar* artist, and Barry Appleby.

There were new names amongst the officials too. Maurice Hudlass, who succeeded his inventor-father Felix as Chief Engineer of the RAC, and a certain L.V. Russell, of whom more anon.

In the Rally programme, a policeman was recommending Standard cars − a Little Nine cost £159 − in contrast to the previous year's sales drive for the world's fastest baby car (tooled along by George Eyston at something like 118 mph). Also in the programme, was an advertisement for a crime novel, The Motor Rally Mystery, which, if nothing else, proved that some enterprising author had been quickly off the mark.

Again there were starting points all over the British Isles but this time the finish was to be at Hastings. The thousand-mile road section was almost inevitably pretty uneventful since once again the weatherman was fairly kind. True, there was some steady rain with a consequent affect upon the 'electrics' but this and a few patches of fog here and there was insufficient to prevent more than 32 of the original 340 starters reaching the finishing point where re-starting on a gradient was added to the slow-running, acceleration and braking tests.

Indeed, the main furore seemed to concern the question of what to wear? Some saloon-drivers were in shirt-sleeves but those at the wheel of open sports-cars were often garbed like Arctic explorers with flying-helmets, fur collars et al. And as for the ladies, there were even some who had the temerity to wear trousers. It would be hard to do better than quote from a comment in *The Motor:*

'Not a few of the women drivers found trousers warmer than skirts and there were a few amusing cases of mistaken identity due to this cause. At the final control, for instance, an official was expressing his view of the appalling weather in no uncertain terms, imagining that the flannel-trousered legs protruding from the door of a small car belonged to a man. Judge his confusion when the wearer of the trousers turned out to be a girl!'

Of course, that poor official would probably be even more confused today. The wearer of a skirt might turn out to be a man!

The Hastings publicity department was no more fortunate than Torquay had been the year before. Rain fell without pause during the three hour period in which the competitors checked in and, again quoting, 'great waves beat noisily on the shore'. And, alack and alas, for Hastings, it continued to rain throughout the final tests and until the organisers decided to hold the concours under cover in the great underground car park. Then, with the normal perversity of the English climate, the sun did break through – but it was too late to change the arrangements.

Crashed gears, burning clutches and all sorts of minor mishaps featured in the final tests but the only near-catastrophe occurred when Mike Couper's Riley caught fire – due to a rag soaked in oil having been tied around the exhaust-pipe. Couper, a prominent Monte Carlo Rally competitor, was to establish quite a reputation as a specialist in picking up Concours awards – when, needless to say, rags were not tied around his exhaust pipe.

When the smoke had cleared, the winner of Class One (over 16 hp) was T.D. Weston, in a Rover; of Class Two (10 to 16 hp), Kitty Brunell, AC; and of Class Three (under 10 hp), G. Dennison, Riley. But perhaps of most

Harry Kallstrom (pronounced Shellstrom and nicknamed the Sputnik) clutches the winner's trophy....the Peall Trophy is, in fact, a cup originally awarded for the world billiards championship and named after champion W.J. Peall....

interest to the future story of the RAC Rally was that classified 76 out of the 106 finishers in Class Three was the man who was to play the major role in the post-war years of putting the RAC on the international rally map: J.H. Kemsley (Riley) starting from Norwich.

Thus was the pattern set for a series of highly-successful events only terminated by the outbreak of war.

The finishing point was switched from year to year and occasionally some of the starting-points were changed too but, by and large, the formula remained constant – 1,000 miles on the road followed by tests to sort out the final positions. Captain Phillips and his helpers waxed more lyrical in their attempts to attract entries (competitors in 1934 were invited to share 'the delicious pains and more delicious pleasures') but it seemed to work for, with a limit of 400 cars, no less than 450 entries were received.

Blackpool saw the start of many an RAC Rally both pre-war and after....Ake Anersson (SAAB) sets off from the Imperial Hotel in strong winds and heavy rain

37

And the entry-lists read like a 'Who's Who' of motoring. In 1934, John Gott appeared in the lists, later to be the captain of the BMC Rally Team, a production car racing champion, Vice-Chairman of the RAC Competitions Committee and – in working life – Chief Constable of Northamptonshire. Another starter from the same control at Leamington was William Shakespeare, believe it or not. And the indefatigable J.H. Kemsley this time began his odyssey from Buxton.

Manufacturers were beginning to take the Rally very seriously indeed. There was a special award for them by now, the Lord Wakefield of Hythe Trophy, and by 1934, there were some fifteen manufacturers officially sponsoring entries: AC, Armstrong Siddeley, Aston Martin, Alvis, Citröen, Ford, Riley, Rover, Singer, SS, Standard, Sunbeam, Triumph, Lagonda and Marendaz.

The Rally moved on to Eastbourne in 1935 and amongst the interesting 'new' names were Bob Gerard, gallant upholder of British motor racing in the pre-Vanwall, Connaught and Cooper period; Alan Hess, a PRO with a penchant for long-distance record-breaking; 'Goff' Imhof; S.M. Lawry, a

Water jump 1....

Water jump 2....

Water jump 3....

The RAC invites 'Join Here' but the navigator of this Mini is in rather a rush....

....but have they been lucky after all? Someone appears to be signing on....

familiar figure as starter of many modern motor-races; W.A. McKenzie, for a long time motoring correspondent of the *Daily Telegraph*; rally and trials expert Denis Flather; Stanley Sears, famous father of a famous son, Jack, noted saloon car racer; and that pawky Scot, the late John Eason Gibson, outstanding administrator of the Silverstone circuit but then a lean hawkish figure in a flying helmet.

It was estimated that even at thirties' prices, some £150,000 worth of motor car took part in that year's Rally. And, after all, you could get a Morris Eight for £118.

It was back to Torquay the following year and the manufacturers battle was now joined by Clement-Talbot, Fiat, Hillman, Humber, Railton, Wolseley and Squire in addition to the others. Harold Nockolds, later to be motoring correspondent of *The Times* and Editor of *The Motor*, appeared in the entry lists as did R.D. Poore, Dudley Noble, Rodney Walkerley and Sir Ronald Gunter. And who could protest at the quality of the poetry ('it isn't for the honour and glory or aught that matters a sight, it's the love of a bit of adventure that's speeding us out to the night') when it continued to pull in so many entries?

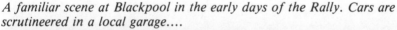

A familiar scene at Blackpool in the early days of the Rally. Cars are scrutineered in a local garage....

Hastings again in 1937 with Lord Austin himself, Norman Garrad, team-manager extraordinary with Sunbeam, Tommy Wisdom, Brian Lewis, Mike Cooper, Goff Imhof, Joan Richmond, Denis Flather and R.D. Poore in the lists and HRG and MG coming forward to contend the Manufacturers Award.

Blackpool, focal point of many post-war rallies, became the finish for the first time in 1938. Jensen, Austin and Frazer-Nash were amongst the team entries and two well-known journalists, the one and only Laurie Cade, of the *Star,* and Basil Cardew, later of the *Daily Express,* were amongst the individual contenders. Despite the war clouds looming on the horizon, the 1939 Rally went ahead as planned. The finish was at Brighton with headquarters at the Metropole Hotel (shades of the Emancipation Day Run) but by now the number of starting points had been limited to London, Torquay, Blackpool and Stratford.

There were 224 entries and for far too many of them it would be the last motor rally in which they would compete.

But before the curtain comes down on that first act of the RAC Rally, let's take a look at some of the highlights of those pre-war years...

Pardon, My Slip is Showing

IN ONLY one of the pre-war RAC Rallies did the weather truly test the driving and navigational skills of the competitors. This was in 1937, when conditions were so bad that the event was nicknamed the Arctic Rally.

Drivers had to battle against snow, ice, torrential rain, sleet and dense fog to reach the finishing point at Hastings. And when they did get there, the sea was so fierce, breaking high over the promenade, that some of the final tests had to be scrubbed.

Surprisingly and despite the conditions, competitors rose magnificently to the occasion and of the 192 starters only eight failed to finish, a much lower proportion than normally when weather conditions were much better.

For once, the background to the start was more in keeping with what was to become a familiar scene in post-war rallies... 'deep snow in Yorkshire'... 'Porlock Hill blocked'... 'impassable under eight-feet snowdrifts'... and so on. In the sequel, Porlock was not impassable. An enthusiastic RAC member took the trouble to make a personal inspection of the hill before the competing cars were due then telephoned the Club to give the true situation which was that Porlock itself was clear despite the snow on the surrounding hills.

One of the few cars which did fall victim to the weather was the Talbot driven by Alan Hess which skidded on ice near Oxford and crashed into a wall. Although Alan is a publicity man by profession it was presumably coincidence that his co-driver was the BBC's commentator for the event. At least, the Corporation must have got one thrilling eye-witness account out of the Rally.

Forced out of the Rally by a similar incident which also culminated in a clash with a bridge, C.M. Hawley (Aston Martin) bought a Morris locally for £50 and proceeded merrily on his way to Hastings.

Although year after year, the Press congratulated the RAC on its smooth organisation, officials did not always escape stricture. Many people took a dim view of an incident in the 1933 event when Mrs. J. Cliff (MG Magna) was penalised for early arrival at the finish. Her story was that she was waiting outside the control when an RAC man peremptorily waved her in. An incident which had echoes many years later when competitors complained that a direction sign had been obscured by a policeman standing in front of it.

The marshals officiating on the slow-running tests of the 1933 Rally also came under fire. They had to sit beside the drivers to observe fair play and a motoring magazine acidly commented 'they were very backward in coming forward when they were required to sit in open cars in the drenching rain'.

And who shall blame them?

One has the feeling too that the judges of the coachwork competition that year did not meet with the full approval of the Press. First prize in one class went to M.L. Curtis (V8 Ford) whose vehicle was cellulosed red and black after the style of Chinese lacquer-work. The instrument board was enormous and studded with giant dials and the car also had a tail-fin like the record-breaking Bluebird. 'Few motorists would have the moral courage to drive in it,' said *The Motor*.

On the other hand, the alertness and vigour of some officials the following year met with unrestrained approval. Vis: 'Bunny Dyer, the starter in the first test, was too alert to let those competitors who tried a rolling start get away with it.' And: 'Reuben Harveyson was a vigorous starter in the second test. He hit the ground so hard with the wooden flag each time, that an appreciable hole was dug in the road surface.'

But there were portents that year of the ever-increasing competition in rallies and the troubles which would ensue in the future over regulations and the interpretation thereof.

It was reported that there was a lot of organised assistance for various competitors en route although this was not permitted by the regulations. It was also alleged that many of the so-called standard cars were not so very standard after all, judging by the performances they put up.

Even less popular than the officials were the police, who were especially active during the 1935 Rally. Three police vans were busy near Glossop on the Buxton route and Huddersfield police were also on the warpath, a

The rally car has brought about many innovations from the very start of the RAC....and this is the 'works department' of the modern Triumph TR7 rally car

competitor in a Bentley being caught by police in a plain van. A Morris was also stopped just outside Huddersfield.

The official programme at Llandudno carried a welcome to motorists. It didn't specify what sort of welcome. Here, the local police laid on the reception committee and had their own gala night. One speed trap alone collected 17 competitors.

It was presumably to make the Rally cars less conspicuous that in 1939, the organisers substituted small labels on the windscreen for the big rally plates the cars had previously carried.

For it is a fact that to some people the mention of a Rally is like a red rag to a bull and rally-drivers are often blamed for incidents which are nothing to do with them.

Only a few years ago, during an RAC Rally, a senior police official telephoned me from a West Country town and requested the name and address of a rally competitor who had been seen driving recklessly through the town. Despite his far from courteous manner, I replied in a friendly **45** fashion and asked if he was sure that it was a rally car since the route of the event went nowhere near his town! Yes, it was a rally car and that was that. So, I said, give me the competition number of the car and I will be able to look up the driver's name and address. No, he didn't have the competition number of the car but – triumphantly – he could describe it. It was a grey Jaguar. Then it wasn't a rally car, said I, since there are no grey Jaguars entered. Well, perhaps it wasn't grey. It doesn't matter whether it was grey or sky-blue pink, said I, since there isn't a Jaguar of any description taking part in this Rally. End of conversation.

What with officials and policemen, you would think that competitors had enough troubles. But not a bit of it. We are forgetting the animal kingdom.

Two Scottish starters in the 1934 event, Mrs Pringle and Mrs Hylton, were lucky to escape death when they swerved to avoid a dog near Bristol and crashed into a wall. Both were taken to hospital injured. Another crew the same year claimed to have had a terrific fight with an eagle in the Scottish mountains – but they had difficulty in finding listeners to believe their story.

More people were prepared to believe the chap who said he had been delayed by a recaltritant cow which lay down in the middle of the road and refused to move. It certainly came true in 1979 when Stig Blomqvist's Saab collided with a cow en route to the start.

The lovely Miss Daniell, who ran out of oil on Shap the previous year, strenuously denied the story circulating that she rode into the nearest village on the back of a passing goat. In 1934, there would have been plenty of oil available on Shap. The road was swimming in the stuff after a load fell off a lorry and caused 'fun and games' for the following rally cars.

As for Miss Daniell and the goat, well, Tommy Wisdom was reported to have continued his journey on an ox after crashing one year in the Monte.

Fun was a doubtful description in some cases and the motoring reporters of the thirties tended to be extremely critical of some of the competitors. J.A. Driskell, competing in the 1933 event, 'drove a blue sports model 8 hp Ford with his crew attired to match, but he could not live up to it all; he was very cautious in applying the brakes and then overran the line, whilst to cap matters, he crashed the gears terribly as the car accelerated.' And the same writer, talking about a gentleman without whom the modern RAC Rally would not be the great international event it is: '...the immense entry of Rileys, the majority of which were obviously in the hands of skilful drivers. Unfortunately for one, J.H. Kemsley, his engine did not appear to be warmed up to do its job sufficiently and spat back repeatedly.'

Innovations outside the regulations are carefully checked....but all seems well as Rauno Aaltonen and his Datsun pass the scrutiny of veteran scrutineer S. Proctor....

Jack K. was not the only personality to have his troubles. Leading motor dealer Charles Follett ran into fog on the 1935 Rally, took a bend too sharply then ran into a wall. Result: no injuries to the occupants but a very badly-dented Speed Twenty Alvis which would certainly have looked out of place in the elegant Follett showrooms.

This was the year when the Mayor of a certain town en route apparently stayed up beyond his usual bedtime to greet the first arrival but after delivering an address of welcome, promptly retired. The remaining competitors received a note from the Mayor plus a box of ginger biscuits from a local firm.

Nowadays, it is difficult to realise just how much those 1,000 mile jaunts across the British Isles were expeditions across comparatively unknown territory. During the 1936 Rally, competitors coming in from the Fens were confused by the sign-posting in that neck of the woods. At Sleaford, a sign said Kings Lynn was 18 miles. The next said 16. A mile on, the sign went back to 18 and then 15 and 16 followed.

Fuel injection on a rally engine....the TR7 V8

Below *The Ford Escort RS 1800... the most successful RAC Rally car of all time*

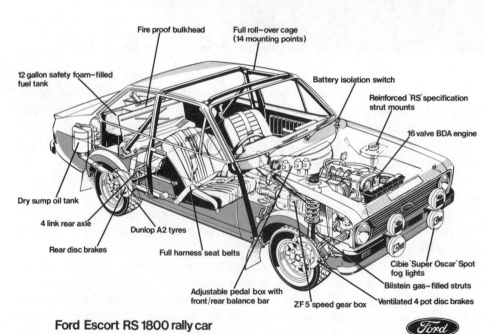

Fire proof bulkhead

Full roll–over cage (14 mounting points)

12 gallon safety foam–filled fuel tank

Battery isolation switch

Reinforced `RS` specification strut mounts

16 valve BDA engine

Dry sump oil tank

4 link rear axle

Dunlop A2 tyres

Rear disc brakes

Full harness seat belts

Cibie `Super Oscar` Spot fog lights

Bilstein gas–filled struts

Adjustable pedal box with front/rear balance bar

ZF 5 speed gear box

Ventilated 4 pot disc brakes

Ford Escort RS 1800 rally car

Ford

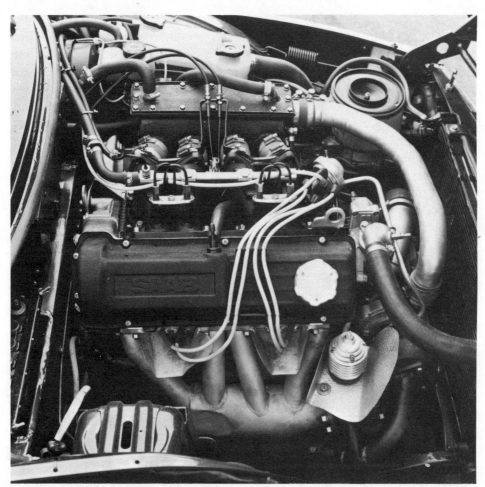

In 1979 SAAB became the first rally entrant to use a turbocharged engine. The blown two-litre produces 145 bhp in standard form and modified for rallying it produces 270 bhp

Come to think of it, there are still some signs like that on British roads today.

The London route on the same Rally gave many drivers their first look at the Mersey Tunnel. One driver, seeing pegs marking the traffic lanes, comforted himself with the thought that if he hit them they were only made of wood. It is probably just as well that he did not hit them − they were, in fact, iron.

THE STORY OF THE RAC INTERNATIONAL RALLY

The Rally obviously brought opportunity to some enterprising folk. There were complaints that a Glasgow garage charged 12s 6d (62.5p) for washing competitor's cars – a cheap enough charge today but one calculated to make the washer a millionaire in 1936. Enterprise sometimes met with peculiar rewards, however. Goff Imhof had an open Singer Nine which he converted into a saloon by means of an elegant celluloid top. This was too much for some wag at the Yarmouth start who chose a moment when the car was unattended to fill it with aspidistras and palms to make it a truly mobile conservatory.

To the good folk of East Anglia, the Rally must have been a mixed blessing and at least one local inhabitant undoubtedly preserved decided views on such things for many a long year.

Peter Clark (Jensen-Ford V8 Special) was groping his way along the fog-bound Newmarket Road with the aid of spotlights focussed outwards on to each margin of the road. Suddenly he heard a faint screeching noise and thought that there was something wrong with the car. Judge his embarrassment on discovering that the noise came from a cyclist hidden in the fog between the two beams and who, with the Jensen's radiator only a foot behind his posterior, was pedalling for dear life to get away.

Also in the red face category were a number of incidents on the 1938 Rally. Amongst the favourites were two drivers with excellent rally records, Tommy Wisdom, driving an SS100, and J. Whalley (Ford V8). Whalley suffered from engine failure in the middle of a test then made matters worse by hitting a barrier whilst the elegant Tommy, usually the personification of coolness, engaged reverse by mistake on the starting-line and shot backwards into a parked car.

Less obviously embarrassing since it didn't take place in full view of the public, was the 'black' put up by a navigator in another car. After carefully directing his driver for over an hour until they wound up in a place miles off the rally route, he discovered that he had been following the line of the county border instead of the route which he had outlined before the start in ink. The comments of his driver have not been recorded for posterity.

And then there was Count Heyden and his Delahaye. Well ahead of schedule as he neared Blackpool, the Count decided to stop for a leisurely lunch and then drive into the control dead on time. He enjoyed his lunch then went outside to discover a tyre was flat. Discovery No. 2 was that his jack wouldn't work. Which is how early arrival becomes late ditto on a rally.

Yet it wasn't all fun and games. The pre-war RAC Rallies produced many
ideas for improvements in ordinary motor cars, developments in heating

And there have even been improvements for the Press. Mobile Press Room as seen on the RAC....

systems and so on, which have helped the comfort of the motorist today. Interior heaters, which, when the Rally was first held, were fitted only to one or two of the more expensive motor cars, soon became almost standard equipment. Radios began to appear in the cars — and on the Rally these were particularly useful for getting up-to-date weather reports and so on. Shades of the BBC Motoring Unit today. Many and ingenious were the methods designed to combat foggy conditions ranging from whole batteries of special lamps to simple yellow discs. In one instance, discs made of the outer husks of onions were carried, the driver insisting that the amber tint so produced was extremely effective.

A good example of what could be done was a four-door saloon Rolls-Royce entered for the 1933 Rally by C.W. Ward. A class-winner in the Concours, it 'bristled with neat and practical features'. These included deep recesses in the backs of the front bucket seats to accommodate stationery and a lady's companion set, access to which was obtained by extending the folding picnic tables. Fitted within the body was a Clayton combined fan and water heater which could be used to circulate warm air in winter and cool in summer.

51

Six years later, even a Triumph roadster in the event carried an electric razor. Packed with even more features than the Rolls-Royce, although hardly so elegant, was an 18 hp Wolseley which had recently been on a record-breaking run to the Cape. Unfortunately, during this run, the car had fallen off a bridge and so it looked somewhat out of place in the Coachwork Competition of the RAC Rally. There was scarcely an undented panel and the doors were packed with sacking where they had been twisted out of shape. Nevertheless, the car carried a great deal of interesting equipment and a good but simple device consisted of green celluloid strips which could be attached to the windscreen by means of suction caps and so cut out the glare from the sun, no matter from what angle.

Other cars were fitted out with interior windscreen wipers which could be folded away when not in use, illuminated map-reading glasses, universally-adjustable front seats, electrically-operated rear-blinds, transparent roof panels and tool trays beneath the boot lids.

But full marks go to a Wolseley which incorporated a bed, a wash-basin and a canteen – and obviously deserved the description of a travelling flat. And before you laugh, note if you will that one of the features of the Austin Maxi, introduced in 1969, was – a bed.

And a final neat touch was added by the Rolls-Royce Wraith of car dealer-cum-Brooklands racer Jack Barclay. Not only did the Wraith carry a cigar-box, flask, clothes brush and writing-pad but, delicatesse upon delicatesse, a backgammon board.

And then the Balloon Went up

THE EIGHTH – and as it was to prove – last RAC Rally before the Second World War, took on a new complexion. For the first time there were only four starting-points: London, Blackpool, Stratford-upon-Avon and Torquay. The London starters went into Wales and then via Southport to Scarborough; from Blackpool, competitors drove into Scotland and then returned to Scarborough; the Stratford starters also reached the Yorkshire seaside town via Wales; while those from Torquay went by way of East Anglia.

All four routes were due to converge at Scarborough in the early hours of Wednesday, the road section having begun at noon the previous day. Then from Scarborough, the surviving cars headed across the Yorkshire moors to Buxton for an overnight stop. Next day they left for the South, taking in the Cowdale hill-climb en route to Aylesbury and the final control before the finish at Brighton.

The routes were all about 850 miles in length (compare approximately 2,500 postwar) with the Stratford contingent covering the longest distance – 866 – and the Londoners the shortest 823.

Although the weatherman provided a mixed-bag (sunshine, biting cold winds, snow, hail and rain were all reported) few competitors ran into trouble and most had time to spare at Aylesbury and a consequent easy run into Brighton. Two of the ladies did meet an 'untimely end', however. A Miss Brotchie, driving an Atlanta, sustained a broken back-axle (the Atlanta, not Miss Brotchie) while Miss Streather (SS) failed to stop when a non-competing car did so in front of her. Result – a rather large insurance claim.

53

*Hangover from 1939 to the immediate post-war rallies were the trousers and
pullovers worn by the crews. Then someone invented rally jackets....*

With the gift of hindsight it is easy to see that the Rally's present course
was an invitation to disaster and something would have to be done to make
life tougher for the competitors.

Although it might be argued that the format of the event gave the
ordinary amateur driver a fair chance, there were already indications that the
Rally was becoming more and more dominated by those who, if not strictly
professional, were engaged in the motor industry or trade. And with an easy
road section culminating in performance tests, many of the leading drivers
were better-known as stars of the race track.

But for spectators, sensible rally dress has remained the same....something to keep out the rain, snow, fog and anything else the weatherman can dream up

And also remaining the same is the willingness of spectators to come to the aid of anyone who lands in a ditch....which is not unknown

Indeed, when the results of the 1939 Rally were worked out, the best performance of all had been given by the well-known trials and racing-driver, A.F.P. Fane, in a two-seater Frazer-Nash-BMW, with another fine effort coming from H.J. Aldington, who was the managing-director of the concern marketing those cars. In fact, the Frazer-Nash team swept the board, gaining revenge for the victories achieved by the SS team in recent rallies.

Works cars dominated the smaller classes too with the Morgan four-wheelers triumphant, all driven by members of the Morgan company. Again the boss showed how it should be done with H.F.S. Morgan himself winning

56

the class for closed cars up to 10 hp.

The dominance of those actively engaged in the commercial side of motoring extended even to the coachwork competition where Jack Barclay again gained pride of place.

The buds of May were upon the land and the following May was to see blossom of a different kind, the blooming mushrooms of ack-ack and exploding shells, the rattle of bullets and the crimson flowers of war staining the map of Europe and eventually of the world. Under the circumstances, it is hardly surprising that many of the 224 entries in the 1939 RAC would not again figure in the lists of motor-sport events. Some died in the service of their country and others, by the time the war ended, had been wearied of such things by the burden of the years.

Some few names remained to play their part in the revival of motor sport after the war. Looking down those 224 entries, one sees W.A. McKenzie, who as mentioned earlier was to be the motoring correspondent of the *Daily Telegraph* for many years: Stanley Barnes, later to be Competitions Manager of the RAC and in more recent years, technical adviser to the Mobil Economy Run; Sammy Davis, Sports Editor of *The Autocar* and prominent racing-driver; Tommy Wisdom, motoring correspondent of the *Daily Herald* and later Chief Executive of the British School of Motoring; and Alan Hess, record-breaker and PRO for Simms Motor Units at one time.

Then there was Raymond Mays, driving a sports-car of that name. The Mays cars were well-received but little else appears in the records about them. Their designer has achieved rather more fame as the man behind the ERA, which so valiantly upheld British motor-racing prestige before the war; and the BRM which, after many vicissitudes, eventually proved a Grand Prix winner in more recent times.

And there was one car which did not complete the tests which was, however, to play a prominent role in the sporting event being prepared by that well-known Clerk of the Course, A. Hitler Esq. This was a little American Bantam – with which many uniformed posteriors were to become well-acquainted during hostilities.

In the coachwork competition, classes were divided this year by price and it may be of interest to the modern reader to know what those prices were.

There were three classes for cars costing less than £200 and the winners in these categories included BSA, Austin, Vauxhall and Hillman. There were a further three classes covering cars between £201 and £350 and here the winners were MG, Talbot, Riley and SS. Next came cars between £351 and £600 and here Triumph, Daimler and again SS dominated.

57

There was one class for cars from £601 to £1,000, won by Daimler, and one class for cars over £1,000, won (surprise, surprise) by Rolls-Royce with Lagonda second.

By the time the RAC Rally achieved international status in the post-war years, cars were to cost just a little more. And many of us were regretting refusals of those snazzy sports-cars offered to us at knockdown prices by friends posted to faraway places.

But then a lot of things would be different after the war...

The Ladies, God Bless 'em

SHOCKED though some Rally stalwarts may have been by the emergence of females in trousers, they simply had to live with them – in the motor competition sense, that is. Rallying has had a great appeal to the sporting female from the beginning of its story, perhaps because here was one field of endeavour where a top-class woman exponent of the art could hold her own with most men.

The fifteen entries from the Womens Automobile Sports Association in the very first RAC Rally of all set a precedent which scores of daring females have followed with gusto.

In 1933, there were no less than 65 women entrants and one of them, Kitty Brunell, won her class in an AC Ace tourer. In Kitty's case, it ran in the family. Her father, a Press photographer whom I knew in later years, had driven in the winning car in the 1926 Monte Carlo Rally.

Mrs Daniell, in another AC, won her class in the coachwork competition and the womens' team of which both formed a part, was runner-up for the team award. The others in the team were Barbara Daniell, whom we have met before, a pretty girl who was the motor-sport 'pin-up' of her day, and Dorothy Champney, who had better luck than when hitting a telegraph pole the previous year.

Amongst the big cars, the Hon. Mrs Chetwynd (Ford) was fourth in her class, Fay Taylour (Ford) sixth and Robina Maugham (Ford) 22nd. Of the eleven girls who started in Rileys, every one finished.

But there were obviously some difficulties confronting women entrants which were not experienced by the men.

Of Mrs Gripper, who drove a Delage with an all-woman crew, a magazine report laconically commented: 'Any chance that she may have had of doing well on the tests was ruined by the distracting chatter of her passengers'.

Presumably, back-seat drivers have been with us a long time.

Woman rally-drivers at that time were also a danger to their relatives. Another crew in the same event lunched with relations in Chester, dined with friends in Torquay and slept for a couple of hours at the home of another relative.

Fortunately, time schedules in the modern RAC Rallies prevent such visitations.

But don't run away with the wrong ideas. There were some pretty tough women drivers in those pre-war rallies and the best of them gave the men drivers all the competition they needed. Nor were they lacking in determination – a Miss Streather, whose Alvis was badly damaged, still pressed on in the 1935 Rally and managed to reach her control at Truro, the sort of incident that could be repeated ad lib where the girls were concerned.

Amongst the outstanding women drivers of the time were Mrs Alfred Moss and Mrs 'Bill' Wisdom, which probably accounts for the fact that in post-war RAC Rallies – and other major international events for that matter – one of the outstanding women teams of all times was – Pat Moss and Ann Wisdom, yes, the daughters of Mrs M. and Mrs W.

Another pre-war woman competitor was the famous airwoman Amy Johnson, who drove in the 1938 Rally. The rally route took in Tenby from where Amy Johnson had started her Atlantic flight and half the population turned out to see her in the new guise of motor rally driver.

But back to Mrs Moss. Read this description of her efforts on the 1936 Rally if you want to know from where daughter Pat got her extraordinary ability at the wheel of a rally car:

'Probably the most spectacular and, incidentally, one of the best-judged climbs of the day was made by Mrs A.E. Moss (Marendaz Special); she threw her car about with utter abandon, finally, disappearing round the hairpin in a great tail skid, with a razor-edged exhaust note which would have done credit to a fighting plane.'

She did, in fact, make best performance of the day with a time much better than anyone else in the Rally, men included.

Not surprisingly, Mrs Moss has always retained her interest in the RAC Rally. I remember one year when, for some reason, she took to phoning me round 2 o'clock every morning for news of Pat's progress. She was so keen and so polite about it that I didn't have the heart to tell her that I was trying to snatch a few hours sleep in between newspaper editions and radio bulletin deadlines. So, until she reads this, she will never have known.

The post-war period has produced a whole crop of top-flight women rally drivers. From the Continent have come Ewy Rosqvist (Sweden), Annie Soisbault (France) and Sylvia Osterberg (Sweden) amongst others. And the home countries have unearthed a succession of winners: Sheila Van Damm, Nancy Mitchell, Anne Hall, Pat Moss and Rosemary Smith, for example.

Pat Appleyard partnered her husband in his immediate post-war successes and the other dominant woman competitor of the time was Sheila Van Damm. Both, of course, were the daughters of very successful men — although in widely contrasting fields. Pat's father was Sir William Lyons, who built the Jaguar cars Ian drove to victory, Sheila's father was the man behind London's Windmill Theatre, home of 'girlie' shows where the proud boast was that despite the blitz the capital endured during the war, 'we never closed'. Sheila was undoubtedly the top woman competitor of her time and a star of the Rootes team.

Marie-Claude Beaumont, European Ladies Champion, 1972

But coming to the front were a couple of other English women who were to stay in the top rank for some years — Nancy Mitchell and Anne Hall.

Nancy, she of the auburn hair and winning smile, was not only a great competitor but one of the nicest people in the sport although on occasion, like all rallying folk, she could give her views in no uncertain fashion. Wife of a High Wycombe doctor, she continued her great interest in the sport after herself giving up international competition and has, on a number of occasions, been an official of the RAC Rally.

Anne Hall had an even more remarkable record of success than Nancy. From the time she partnered her sister in a Jaguar on the 1951 RAC, this forceful Yorkshire housewife and mother really made an impact — sometimes literally as when she turned the car over at the Nurburgring during a Tulip Rally. At various times she co-drove with Nancy Mitchell, Sheila Van Damm, and Valerie Domleo, her greatest successes coming after she joined the Ford works team in 1957.

Then she certainly proved that she was as good if not better than many of the leading men drivers. In the 3,000 miles of scrub, sand and rock which makes up the East African safari, she finished third overall, a tremendous performance for a woman.

That year she also won the Ladies Prize in the Monte, following-up her victories in the RAC.

After the Safari she landed at London Airport, gave a Press conference, picked up her car and drove to London's Connaught Rooms where she and I were judging a car competition for a cornflake manufacturer (what heady lives we lead to be sure!). Naturally, I congratulated Anne on her Safari achievement and was a little surprised when she said, 'I was a bit unpopular with Ford's. They wanted me to take it steadily to make sure of the Ladies Prize instead of going all-out to finish as high as I could. So I told them if that was all they wanted they could get someone else to drive.'

And I was even more surprised when Anne, as soon as the judging was completed, said she must be off to the Midlands, to take part in the *Birmingham Post* Rally due to start that evening.

No, Anne Hall didn't know the meaning of 'take it steadily'. Afterwards she became a driving instructor but every year she pays a visit to the RAC Rally.

Anne's ascendancy was eventually threatened by a partnership, Pat Moss and Ann Wisdom, which could surely lay claim to be one of the greatest rally combinations of all time. Indeed Pat's record of having won the Ladies Prize in the RAC Rally no less than eight times is unlikely ever to be beaten.

The greatest of all the lady drivers, Pat Moss with RAC Chairman, Wilfrid Andrews, after her 1965 victory

Anne Hall talking to John Sprinzel

The glamorous Ewy Rosqvist pauses for refreshment

*Pauline Mayman, BMC
works driver*

Competition was in the blood with both. Some of Mrs Moss's rallying exploits are recounted elsewhere in these pages and father Alfred was racing at Indianapolis long before brother Stirling's bright light hurtled across the motor-racing scene. Tommy and 'Bill' Wisdom were outstanding rally and race drivers too, with 'Bill' holding the outright lap record at Brooklands, a remarkable achievement for a woman.

Ann partnered Pat in most of the latter's big wins although she retired from rallying after her marriage to another leading competitor, Pete Riley. Big, blond Pete always sticks in my memory for a somewhat unusual reason. Many years ago on a rally we were 'lost'. The tail-lights of another car came into view and with delight we saw from the competition plates that it was Pete Riley's car. 'He must know where he's going,' said I and off we went in pursuit. We followed Pete for mile after mile – and then he turned into an all-night café. He had retired from the rally an hour previously and was just driving around looking for some much-needed eggs and bacon. Collapse of stout party.

But to get back to Pat Moss. If Anne Hall gave the men something to think about, Pat proved that a woman rally driver could be as good as any man. Ladies Prizes have been incidental to her for most of her career since she became the first woman to win a European Championship event outright when she took the honours in the 1960 Liège-Rome-Liège which was, incidentally, one of the toughest events in the world at that time. The year before she had been second in the German Rally, that same year she was second in the Alpine and the following year second in the RAC. So you can see that Ladies Prizes were small beer indeed to her, a fact she rubbed in by further outright wins in the 1962 German and Alpine events.

The Moss-Wisdom combo drove almost entirely for BMC in the early years – Pat in full flight around a race circuit in the big Healey was quite something – but in 1963 Pat married another popular driver, the big Swede, Erik Carlsson, thrice winner of the RAC Rally. After that year's RAC, she joined the Saab works team for which her husband drove.

Had she not climbed to the top of the rally tree, Pat might have been just as successful as a show-jumper. As it was, she twice toured abroad with British teams and twice placed second in the Queen Elizabeth Cup.

To me, one of the most remarkable things about her was that success left her unspoiled. She has always had time for questioners – and believe me some of the questions put to rally-drivers at various times would win prizes for fatuousness – and has always been ready to co-operate in anything for the good of the sport. I recall once asking her to appear right away on a television programme. She had just driven into the overnight halt at Blackpool, tired from a long drive through the Lake District from Scotland. Many drivers would have told me just where to go but not Pat. Unhesitatingly she agreed. And the point about it is that she would have been just as unhesitating if the request had come from a small boy seeking autographs.

Rosemary Smith, glamorous as ever for the start of the 1965 Rally   67

It isn't all glamour. Rosemary Smith (Hillman Imp) in action

Although, by and large, British girls have dominated the ladies' section in the RAC, there has from time to time been a formidable challenge from abroad. The tall dark Annie Soisbault from France, known to all and sundry as 'Sauceboat', padded across the scene at one time in a female version of a Davy Crockett outfit but it is probably true to say that the best overseas opposition has come from the Swedish girls, Sylvia Osterberg and Ewy Rosqvist.

Sylvia won the unofficial European Championship in 1963, her first full year of rallying, but she had been driving for some twelve years, since she was sixteen. She started in reliability trials for motorcyclists and progressed to stock-car racing. She married a motocross competitor and covered around 35,000 miles a year driving him to and from events. After she took to rallying she had many a fierce tussle with both Pat Moss and Ewy Rosqvist and it is fair to say that any organiser who had these three in the ladies' section could rub his hands at an exciting prospect.

Blonde Ewy started her rally career in 1955 and subsequently picked up a couple of European titles. She drove first with Saab then switched to Volvo before becoming, with Ursula Wirth, the first women's team to drive for the Mercedes 'works' set-up. Both girls were veterinary assistants but were far from the conventional picture of girls who worked on the farm with animals.

Left *Marjatta Aaltonen, sister of European Champion, Rauno. Although Marjatta has driven in the RAC, there is no argument as to who is the best driver in the family – or the best looking...*

Right *Val Domleo, top navigator who married one of the Morley brothers*

Anne Hall (Ford Anglia) at speed in the rain during the Brands Hatch tests of the 1960 Rally. With Val Domleo, she took the Ladies Prize 69

The sight of the glamorous Ewy's bright, tight, blue slacks twinkling across a rain-swept Blackpool promenade was enough to bring a gleam to the most weary competitor's eye.

Talking of glamour, another tall blonde has been a publicity man's dream besides a redoubtable performer for the Rootes team. Rosemary Smith, who must be heartily sick and tired of being described as 'the blonde Dublin dress-designer', has much more than her looks to brighten a team manager's existence. She first enjoyed rally success in her native Circuit of Ireland and was soon afterwards snapped up by Norman Garrad, then manager of the Rootes team. She more than justified his faith and, apart from collecting a bagful of Ladies' Awards, emulated Pat Moss by winning an international event outright, the 1965 Tulip. This was her best year since she also won the Ladies Trophy in the Circuit of Ireland for the third year running, a similar award in the Scottish, was runner-up to Pat Moss in the Monte and took a Coupe des Dames in the GT category of the Alpine Rally.

One of rallying's little mysteries is how Rosemary always arrived at the finishing-line immaculately groomed and looking as fresh as a daisy however gruelling the rally may have been. You might just as well ask how Erik Carlsson always crossed the line in a gleaming shiny red Saab after ploughing through miles of mud. The top drivers, male and female, pay attention to detail.

And you Sunday car-washers would give up in disgust if you could see the quick operation those Saab boys can do on a car and not leave a speck of dust.

In latter years, the number of girls 'starring' in the RAC Rally has been small. Jill Robinson has probably been the most consistent performer whilst France has contributed Marie Claude Beaumont. And the inevitable Pat Moss made a brief comeback one year to win the Ladies Award for Toyota.

These then, are some of the girls who have featured prominently in the RAC Rally. There have been others: Pauline Mayman, Rosemary Seers, Mary Handley-Page, 'Tish' Ozanne and Jennifer Nadin, for instance. All have brought a welcome glamour to the scene; some have proved that international rallying is one sport where, given a chance, a woman can prove just as good as a man.

First of the Many

THE IMMEDIATE post-war years were boom ones for the majority of sports but motor sport took rather longer to get going than most. A noticeable lack of suitable machinery was a great handicap and a weird variety of vehicles took part in many events. Just the same, the RAC was anxious to revive its rally and much behind-the-scenes activity obtained the assurance that in future the RAC Rally would be upgraded from National to International status.

But it was 1951 before it proved possible to run the First RAC International Rally of Great Britain. Despite the official status, the few overseas competitors came mainly from Holland and France, the most notable of these being the redoubtable Marcel Becquart, of Monte Carlo Rally fame. He chose to drive a British car as did most of the foreigners, with the exception of the Germans, who entered a team of Ford Taunus saloons.

Nevertheless, there was an excellent entry of 266 of which, in the sequel, no less than 229 were to start. There were still four starting points, this time Brighton, Cheltenham, Skegness and Harrogate, with a finish at Bournemouth, but in almost every other respect, the Rally was vastly different to its pre-war predecessors. To start with, the time of year was changed and the Rally was held in June. Warm summer weather did nothing to help the event from the severity point of view but the organisers more than made up for this by the rigours of the tests they introduced. These tests, instead of being gathered together at the conclusion of the road section, took place at various points along the route. Actually, this was not a startlingly new innovation – the RAC had adopted a similar procedure for the great 1,000 Miles Trial some fifty years before.

The road section itself was not without difficulty, especially in the Scottish Highlands, where some of the roads and tracks were likened to 'the dried bed of a mountain torrent' and in many places were so narrow that overtaking was impossible. In these conditions was the germ of an idea which was to considerably enhance the Rally in years to come but for the moment officials and competitors alike were living for the present.

All competitors, whatever their starting-point, converged on the Silverstone race circuit for the first test. This comprised driving for half-an-hour around the club circuit at a minimum average speed according to class. This obviously entailed each competitor completing a given number of laps and various ingenious methods were used to count these. Some had a certain number of tear-off sheets of paper and at least one used a book of matches, throwing one away at the end of each lap. Despite this, a large number managed to get their sums wrong. Some of the difficulty was caused by the fact that the entrance to the track was some distance away from the exit and although this was clearly marked, not a few drivers insisted on crossing the line where they had started, thus doing an extra lap and consequently being credited with a slower time.

Whilst all this backstage mathematical juggling was going on, the driving itself was hair-raising. That well-known writer, *Grand Vitesse* commented: 'The speeds were quite fast to watch but what did arouse cries of admiration, not unmixed with fear, was the heeling over of these touring and sports cars, mostly with independent front suspensions, on the sharp turns, notably Stowe Corner. How they could get close to overturning point and remain upright afterwards was most singular. R.F. Batley (Studebaker) had a wheel collapse completely.'

The test certainly created havoc since 114 entrants lost marks and 39 failed completely. It was to give rise to a violent protest from many of the competitors which led to the Stewards deciding at the end of the Rally to delete the Silverstone test from the final results. The official reasons given were that some of the number labels came off the cars and the accuracy of the results was thereby compromised and also that there was room for misunderstanding in the regulations governing that particular test.

Early summer sunshine after the troubles of Silverstone at least gave competitors a chance to enjoy the drive from the Midlands race circuit to Scarborough but once they left the Yorkshire seaside town, darkness swiftly fell as they headed for 'the gateway of the Highlands'. Next day they turned south again and made for Dunoon where they were to get their first night's rest since the start. But they had to earn that rest.

First came a timed stretch over the aptly-named and famous hill-climb course, Rest-and-be-Thankful, where competitors had to equal or improve on standard time to avoid loss of marks.

Again, it would be hard to beat the description of the scene by *Grand Vitesse:*

'From the top of the timed part of the hill it was just possible to see the starter's flat dip as each car got away from the line, down in the green valley below. Then the cars could be seen weaving up the narrow grey road, and the tyres of the faster ones could be heard squealing on the bends a long way below. Ian Appleyard (Jaguar XK120) looked very fast and he slid more than most coming out of the hairpin.'

In the sequel, Ian Appleyard was faster than all, with a time of one minute, 10.5 seconds for the 1,425 yards which I leave to the mathematicians to work out in terms of miles per hour.

To describe Dunoon as a night's rest may, perhaps, be a misnomer because it was at 5 am that the cavalcade resumed its journey towards England. Just outside Carlisle, the late, much-loved Gregor Grant hit a dustcart (just one of the many incidents in his adventurous journalistic-cum-motoring career) but otherwise the next leg passed largely without incident.

The rally organisers had intended that it should be one of the toughest sections of the event with a six-mile timed stretch over the mountain passes of the Lake District but the weatherman did not oblige with the hoped-for wet and misty conditions and in continuing sunshine, most drivers managed well. One Jaguar scraped a rock and a Triumph burst a tyre but only a Studebaker which became completely stuck and had to have outside assistance suffered severely from loss of marks.

So – on to Blackpool and the second overnight halt. But again competitors had to sing for their supper and on the Wednesday evening, the Golden Mile reverberated to the thunder of engines as cars accelerated from a standing start down the promenade, turned right between two pylons, looped to the left around a third pylon, drove back between the first two, continued back up the promenade, turned sharp right between two more pylons, reversed and made a 195 yard dash back to the finishing line, being permitted only 25 yards in which to pull up. Not a recommended exercise for L-drivers and indeed at least one experienced rally driver had his fun-and-games. Mike Couper had to do an emergency stop in his Bentley when a canine gentleman decided to commit suicide. Given a second run because of this incident, Couper found the turn into the finishing straight a bit tight for his big car and hit the sandbags with his nearside front wing.

Bournemouth was a popular finishing point for the RAC. A typical prize presentation outside the Town Hall, on this occasion when Tom Trana (Volvo) won the 1963 event. With the Mayor are John Crampton, RAC Vice-Chairman and Dean Delamont, RAC Competitions Manager

75

Once again, Appleyard was fastest with 36.03 seconds but there was an excellent performance too from Peter Morgan in his Plus Four Morgan, who clocked 37.58. Don 'Pathfinder' Bennett wasn't far behind either with 37.97 in his Jaguar.

The next stage of the Rally was to have special significance in retrospect because the RAC had sought and obtained permission from the War Office to use a military firing range in the Eppynt Mountains. At the time, it was just an exciting innovation in devising new tests for the drivers but it was actually the forerunner of the special stages over Forestry Commission and War Office land which was to make the RAC one of the world's greatest motoring events in later years.

The road to be used was just under two miles long. From a standing uphill start it wound up to a summit, zig-zagged down to a tricky right-hand bend and then snaked uphill again to the top of the moor. Just how tricky the course was can be judged by the fact that the fastest cars only averaged speeds around 56 mph. The Jaguars were again the quickest, V.R. Pilkington clocking 2 minutes, 1.6 seconds, but again Peter Morgan and W.A.G. Goodall did well in their neat little Morgans. And in the under 1.5-litre classes, the Jowetts really came into their own.

One aspect of this special stage would cause heart-failure to Jim Porter and his present-day organisers. The War Office made a condition of loaning the land that other vehicles should be given the right of way if necessary. Which poses the pretty problem: who in 1970 would be more startled — Paddy Hopkirk doing 90 mph on a special stage — or the tank-driver trundling in the opposite direction at 35?

However, all passed without disaster in 1951 and the last day began at 6 am from Weston-super-Mare. What should have been an easy stretch to Launceston turned out anything but since what was described as 'a pride of steamrollers' insisted on their right of way and blocked the main road, causing many of the competitors to make a detour.

And it was just six miles from Launceston that the only fatal accident in the long history of the Rally occurred. J.A. Young, in a sports A40, touched the verge after a bend and crashed. He escaped with only shock and abrasions but his co-driver, D. Parker, was killed.

Bournemouth was crowded as the first of the Rally cars arrived in the town around 2 pm. The sun shone, the place was full of people in summer dress and a final touch was added by HMS Vanguard at anchor in the bay.

From the provisional placings at Bournemouth the final results were still
wide open. The two leaders were Ian Appleyard, who had lost 36.03 marks,

Robin Richards, not to be confused with the broadcaster, a top navigator who served on the Chesham Committee, studies the route ahead as his Volvo is refuelled on the 1962 Rally

and Peter Morgan 37.58, and in every class, there was a similarly close race for the leadership. So all depended upon the final test at Bournemouth on the Saturday.

It proved quite a day. The sun retired from the fray, leaving the promenade course wet and tricky as the mist wafted in from the sea. Drivers had to start when a signal light lit up, accelerate into a chicane 180 yards away, corner, drive 180 yards into another chicane and 180 yards further on again, make a U-turn around a pylon and repeat the whole process on the way back to the starting line. They then had to stop dead within 75 feet.

The outcome was positively hair-raising. Lots of drivers discovered that their brakes were not what they used to be after nearly 2,000 miles of rallying and 'dropping anchor' at 60 mph resulted in broadside skids and officials running for their lives. One car sliced the end of the sandbag wall with great precision and a couple of dozen times or more, pylons went hurtling over, all great sport for the spectators at least.

When the excitement subsided, once again Appleyard's Jaguar and the Morgans of Goodall and Peter Morgan had done well. There was also a good performance from A.G.H. Rimmel in a Healey, unfortunately spoiled by a penalty of five marks for hitting a pylon. Amongst the smaller fry, Becquart's Jowett and Nancy Mitchell's HRG also did well.

The decision was made to eliminate the Silverstone test from the final results as already mentioned but in any case there was little doubt about the best performance in the Rally, that of Ian Appleyard in his Jaguar. Although there was no General Category, the leaders of this class (for open cars over 1,500 cc) would have finished in the same positions overall had there been one – which would have made Appleyard first, Peter Morgan second, Goodall third and Don Bennett fourth. The Morgan team, which was completed by W.S. Steel, won the team prize hands down.

The Motor commented: 'This Rally must become a permanent feature of the calendar, and the organisers are among the first to declare that much has been learned for future events and any mistakes will not be repeated.'

Rally of the Tests

ONE SWALLOW maketh not a summer and by the same token, one Eppynt did not make a 'rally of the forests'. For the next few years after the RAC achieved international status it was to remain very much a 'rally of the tests' with fairly straightforward road sections, save when the weather intervened, interspersed with bursts of furious action on race circuits, hill-climb courses and seaside promenades.

Not surprisingly, the rally was often dominated by drivers of big, fast machinery. Appleyard and his Jaguar were always the combination to beat in those early years with strong opposition from people like Ronnie Adams, Goff Imhof and Don Bennett. One year, Lyndon Sims took the honours in a powerful Aston Martin, the first and only victory for a marque, which, supreme for speed work, was hardly designed for the type of 'forestry commissioning' which was to come later.

The Rally was given a boost for its second year as an international event, the 1952 effort being sponsored by the *Daily Telegraph,* whose motoring correspondent, W.A. Mackenzie, had been a competitor himself in the pre-war days. The starting-time was brought forward to March and this had the desired object of bringing about more difficult weather conditions, at least initially.

Allard cars had seized their chance of glory in the Monte that year and were to repeat their success in the RAC with Imhof winning the open-car class and putting up the best performance irrespective of class.

There was another thrilling struggle between the Jaguar XK120s and the Morgans. Sheer speed and power often gave the Jaguars an edge but the Morgans took the team prize with some comfort.

At the end of the day, some competitors criticised the event for being too easy, others for being too tough. Which goes to show you can't please all of the people all of the time.

The organisers had foreseen this because the programme had this to say:

'Mind you, all dyed-in-the-wool rally drivers have the same mentality; coming out in spots when the weather forecast people recite their messages of gloom and despondency just before the start, yet bursting with vain glory and pride if they finish a rally after battling with fog, mud, ice and snow in unprecedented quantities, therefore pooh-poohing runs in normal conditions as child's play, fit for beginners only.'

Blizzards and deep snow did indeed provide a grim curtain-raiser to the 1952 Rally and the Silverstone stage, ill-fated yet again, had to be cancelled due to the amount of slush on the circuit. But thereafter the weather was mostly reasonable.

The Silverstone cancellation was once more the subject of controversy but the organisers quite rightly did not want to risk a debacle with a multiple pile-up right at the outset. The fatal accident of the previous year must have been still fresh in the memory.

There was a twin start from Hastings and Scarborough and traffic on many main roads was reduced to single line in places owing to snow. The A5 was blocked near Dunstable and many drivers had to make a detour. Imhof was nearly eliminated at this point, being misdirected and covering an extra 30 miles, finally reaching the Silverstone control just in time.

There were blizzards of brief duration during the afternoon before competitors set off for Dorset and then swung up to the Castle Combe race circuit. Here the organisers had fiendishly devised a manoeuvring test in the darkness which sorted out quite a few and a couple retired from the fray.

Through the frosty Welsh night the survivors went on to where the switchback of Eppynt once again awaited them. Something went wrong with the Army telephone system which was being used for rally control and lengthy waits ensued which, in the end, cost many crews the hot baths and meals which awaited them at Llandrindod Wells.

One of the favourites, Maurice Gatsonides (Ford Zephyr) was having trouble with his car and several others dropped out before the crews straggled into Blackpool for the overnight halt. First they had to undergo another test on the promenade and not unexpectedly some very fast times were put up by Appleyard, Imhof and 'Pathfinder' Don Bennett. Not so fast was world professional cycling champion, Reg Harris, trying his hand at four wheels instead of two.

Tests could sometimes be as destructive as forests as R.M. Hall (Sprite) found out on the Wolvey skid-pan

Next day, the route was in to the Lake District for regularity tests. These included a standing start on some of the steepest sections and these really sorted the cars out, more than forty failing in some respect. Gearboxes were damaged, clutches melted and at least one car stuck in first gear and stayed that way for the next 40 miles. Then it was on to Edinburgh and another overnight rest before tackling the famous Rest-And-Be-Thankful hill-climb. Miss Newton, in her Jaguar, was still going like a bomb and put up a time of 1 minute 15 seconds, compared with Appleyard's fastest of the day at 1 minute 11.6 seconds.

On into the boulder-strewn Highlands, deadly on the exhaust pipes of many of the low-slung sports cars, and then back to the Lake District before the final run-in to Scarborough and the last test of all on the Oliver's Mount motorcycle circuit. And when all was over Goff Imhof had won the open class and was best overall with Marcel Becqvart's Jowett victor in the closed class. Morgans were well-deserved team winners and the redoubtable Miss Newton had won the Ladies Award in no uncertain fashion.

The motoring press delivered their verdict: with a little improvement in detail management, the event would take its annual place as one of the big International rallies of the calendar.

There seemed little reason to quarrel with this assertion after the 1953   **81** event. *The Motor* commented: 'There is no doubt that this year's Rally was the best conceived, best planned and best organised of any of the classic RAC Rallies. What looked on paper to be an easy, if not boring, tour round England, Wales and the Lowlands of Scotland from one driving test to another, proved to be one of the most difficult events staged since the war... the foreign competitors found it sufficiently difficult to put them early out of the running.'

Ian Appleyard and his wife Pat once more emerged triumphant in what was described as 'their well-worn and celebrated white Jaguar XK120 two-seater.'

Ian lost no marks on the 1,600 mile road section and made best aggregate in the 11 special tests. Jaguars indeed had a wonderful rally finishing first, fourth, eighth and tenth in the General Category, now officially recognised, and winning the team prize.

Winner of the Touring Class, which counted towards the recently-inaugurated European Championship, was Irish driver, Ronnie Adams, who was to make quite an impact on the international rallying scene during the next few years. With his co-driver, J.R. Pearman, he drove the Sunbeam-Talbot which Stirling Moss, in one of his rare rally appearances, had handled in the Monte, and did well enough to finish second to Appleyard overall. Sheila Van Damm took the Ladies Award after the previous year's winner, Miss Newton, dropped 70 marks at a time control.

What ROSPA and the Ministry of Transport would say nowadays about the Silverstone test one can only conjecture but it was reported that, required to brake hard from 80 mph, 50 per cent of the cars snaked viciously and a few slid broadside on.

It was still very much a rally of the tests as can be gathered from the list:

Silverstone: Half-mile standing start; required to stop within sixty yards of the finishing-line.

Castle Combe: In and out of garages — in darkness.

Prescott: Hill-climb.

Llandrindod Wells: Time test — from a Le Mans start with the drivers sprinting to their cars.

Blackpool: Speed test.

Lakeland: Three hills to be covered in the same time.

Turnberry: Similar to Castle Combe.

Yorkshire Moors: Consistency test similar to Lakeland.

Goodwood: Speed test.

Hastings: Acceleration, garaging and manoeuvre tests (2).

The 1954 event was reckoned even better and certainly tougher. Entries were restricted to standard production touring saloons and standard production sports cars with a handicap based on the average performance of the best 10 cars in each category. That the formula worked was proved by the final outcome: 229 started the 2,000 mile rally and only 164 finished. Of these, only seven had a clean sheet.

It was, no pun intended, a triumph for the new Triumph TR2, Johnny Wallwork finishing first with Peter Cooper second. Behind came Cuth Harrison (Ford) and Peter Harper (Sunbeam-Talbot). Mary Walker, runner-up to Sheila Van Damm in 1953, reversed the order in the Ladies Prize with Nancy Mitchell third. The Morgans were once again the fastest cars on some of the tests but their star driver, Peter Morgan, lost too many marks on the road for the Malvern team to repeat their success in the team competition which went to the Ford team of Harrison, J.G. Reece and Nancy Mitchell.

The twin start was from Hastings and Blackpool and almost everything that could conceivably happen befell the competitors. Thick fog: and drivers lost their way, drove down wrong roads leading into farmyards, found themselves wheel-high in fords of the wet variety, and so on. Two Morgans crashed and a Jowett over-turned. The unkindest cut of all was saved for the redoubtable Goff Imhof. Finding a section blocked by stalled cars, he made a detour only to find that in doing so he had by-passed a secret check. The resultant loss of marks was so heavy that there was little point in him continuing. Not to be outdone, another driver made history on a later section by losing 4,270 marks. More was to come. At the Prescott hill-climb, Sheila Van Damm 'lost it' and slid into a sandbank, the lone Land Rover ran amok and a Volkswagen went over the edge. Maurice Gatsonides crashed into a ditch in the dark and Prince Frederick of Prussia, driving a Porsche, dented his vehicle so much that it was unrecognisable as a Porsche. Despite this, he pressed on to the finish.

Overshadowed in the general classification but putting up a wonderful show nevertheless was the German driver, Schluter, winner of the small-car class in his two-stroke DKW. The remarkable thing about his performance was that he had never previously competed in this country or in a rally of this type.

1955 was tougher still although there was not so much general satisfaction with the outcome. In icy winter conditions, many of the better drivers were baulked by those less skilful than themselves and the final results were only arrived at after all sorts of large-scale amendments.

On the mountains of Wales, the moors of Yorkshire, the hills of **83**

Lakeland, everywhere there was ice. And these stages had to be covered at night — with route directions handed out only at the last moment. The original route soon had to be modified due to deep snowdrifts and some sections of the surviving route were later cancelled and time allowances awarded. This was more than exasperating for those who retired early thinking they had lost too many marks to make it worthwhile continuing only to find that if they had kept going they would have been all right.

Bulldozers and digging teams had to get to work at the Cadwell Park circuit and at Hastings the start was under three inches of ice. Car after car crashed in Wales and the Lake District and just to make the thing really enjoyable, the weather-man sent along a stray blizzard or two. It was all too much for Walter Schluter who gave up, declaring himself exhausted and baffled. Monte winner Sydney Allard hit a bridge and finished with his car tied up with rope, Cuth Harrison collided with a stag in Devon and Frank Grounds went one better by swearing that he had collided with a giraffe!

At Hard Knott Pass, some competitors claimed that the route was impassable but officials trumped their ace. An RAC man in a Morris Minor had got through just ahead of the rally cars so plees for a delay allowance were rejected.

By the time they got back to Hastings about a third of the 238 starters were missing and the rest looked weary, dirty and battered — both cars and crews. Jimmy Ray and B. Horrocks (Standard Ten) were declared the winners by the comfortable margin of 204 marks and Standard with the cars of J.H.B. Dickson and W.K. Richardson making up their trio, took the team award.

Not without significance, a newcomer won her class in the final test at Hastings and put up fifth fastest time of the day. Her name? Pat Moss.

The pattern of tough, rugged sections was repeated in 1956, although there were moments of brilliant sunshine to lighten the way. With the accent on the speed tests the big boys came into their own again and the outright winner was a car big enough to have a crew of three — the Aston Martin of Lyndon Sims, a radio and television shop owner from South Wales. Lyndon was one of the first rally 'stars' I ever met and the friendliness of this quiet, unassuming but very fast driver left an abidingly pleasant recollection. In the years since, of course, I've also met some of the other sort but we won't go into that. Incidentally, star-spotters of the future might have taken a closer look at one of the 1956 winning crew.

The legend 'J. Ambrose' concealed a very young Tony Ambrose, later to

become one of the best co-drivers on the international circuit.

Peter Harper had a great year in 1958 for Sunbeam: winning both a Coupe des Alpes and the RAC International Rally

Jack Sears and Willie Cave check-in at a control on the 1960 Rally. Willie, a BBC producer, did much to get motor sport on the air. Jack became British saloon car racing champion and is now on the RAC Motor Sports Council.

After Lyndon's Aston came – yes, again – the Appleyard Jaguar, Doc Spare's Morgan and another Jag driven by W.D. Bleakley. Peter Cooper's performance in getting his tiny Standard Ten into fifth place was described by one of the motoring magazines as 'a minor miracle'. The same scribe also had a general bouquet to hand out, 'for the robust and healthy little Standard Tens and Renaults and their relatively cramped crews'.

The team award, however, went to three Austins driven by Mrs Johns, Gerry Burgess and Jack Sears. Another Austin, handled by Miss A. Palfrey and Miss A. Jervis, took the Ladies Award, with a Rover, crewed by Mary Handley-Page and Jo Ashfield, second. Jo in later days became a rally official. And third came – Pat Moss and Ann Wisdom. A new era was dawning of outstanding women rally drivers.

Ironically, in view of the Scandinavian domination which was to hit the Rally in the sixties, the best performance by a foreign crew was that of J.D. O'Leary and A.M. Canty and if you wonder how a couple of names like that come to be foreign, they both hailed from the south side of the Irish border which made them citizens of the Republic of Eire.

The 1957 Rally didn't happen. A little bother was going on around the Suez Canal at the time which meant the petrol tankers going a long way round. The consequent rationing put paid to that year's RAC Rally and indeed to a number of other motoring events. It was to be exactly ten years before another Rally was cancelled and that for rather different reasons as shall be told in due course.

1958, however, went on as scheduled with twin starts from Hastings and Blackpool and the finish scheduled for the Sussex town. It was to be the last of the conventional rallies of the tests for reasons apparent in the next chapter.

My then boss, Pat Gregory, went off to Blackpool to handle affairs at that end and I was duly dispatched to Hastings. It was bitterly cold at both ends. One can't say that the rally went without a hitch since just what the hitches were provided a significant change in the basis of the event.

To the outside world, or that section of it concerned with such things, all went well and at the end, although the previous year's winner, Lyndon Sims, was again a strong contender in his Aston, the laurels went to the blond unsmiling Peter Harper, one of the drivers who made the Rootes Competition Department the people to beat in the fifties.

Driving tests were still the main theme and in the cold spring sunshine of Hastings, the scream of tyres and the roar of engines brought hundreds and **86** hundreds of spectators to the promenade. That doyen of motoring

The Suez crisis cancelled the 1957 Rally and petrol prices were rarely out of the news thereafter. A topical comment by 'Gus' of the London Evening News

correspondents, the late, great Laurie Cade, of *The Star,* had other ideas for embryo press officers, insisting that a glass of the best beer in Hastings did wonders for one. Laurie died in 1969, aged 80, and for all who had the honour and pleasure of knowing him well, not only the outstanding motoring journalist of our time but the dearest friend anyone could wish to meet.

That 1958 Rally was also a moment of cheer for John Bullock, who did so much to put Rootes on the press and competition map, John, with the panache for which he is renowned in the motor industry, ensured that the champagne flowed to celebrate a Rootes victory and a 'band of brothers' who were to be together on many RAC Rallies shared in his delight. Memory holds the door to recall Stanley Barnes, so often a trophy winner in the pre-war rallies and later Competitions Manager of the RAC; Vaughan Davies, who left the RAC to mastermind Berkeley in their all too brief foray in the competition world; Laurie Hands, competition manager of Champion spark plugs and a familiar figure at every major motoring event in the world; *87*

Alfred G. Browne, then motoring correspondent of the Press Association: 'Scoop' Russell, boss of the Rally Results Team, who had been an official on every RAC since the very beginning; Cedric Bicknell, Laurie's motoring advertising partner on *The Star;* and many more.

For a 'new boy' it was quite an experience. The only quiet moment of the period was the night before the finish when we were awaiting the return of the cars to Hastings.

Alan Brinton, then motoring correspondent of the ill-fated *News Chronicle,* had been a Parliamentary Gallery reporter before turning to motoring and he reminisced over a pipe and a quiet game of snooker.

Hastings seemed to be deserted and Alan and I the only two moving, breathing things in the town.

On reflection, I don't think I've had a quiet moment on an RAC Rally since.

The other 'moment' was of a rather different character. It occurred on the Sunday morning after the Rally ended. Gregory and Drackett crept down to breakfast feeling decidedly the worst for wear to find that at that early hour, the only other occupant of the room was the then Chairman of the RAC, Wilfrid Andrews. Too late to turn back, we forked half-heartedly at our kidneys and bacon whilst Mr Andrews talked about the most complex aspects of motor sport and, for good measure, world affairs.

If any of the people concerned ever read this, there could be some possible results. 'Scoop' Russell might give me the pound which I won in 'guess how many cars will finish' competition with the others and for which he was the stakeholder: and Alan Brinton might refund the half-crown he won from me whilst he filibustered.

Wilfrid Andrews never apologised for intruding on my headache. He was a very shrewd man and I rather suspect that he knew all along that his PRO and Press Officer had monumental hangovers.

Protesting too much

PRINCESS Margaret never knew but one year she almost put the final 'damper' on the RAC Rally. That was in 1959 and the part the Princess unwittingly played provided a strange last act to one of the most turbulent sequences in the history of the event.

As the sun shone on winner Peter Harper in the previous year, behind the scenes there had been rumblings of discontent. Competitors were, by and large, pretty unhappy about the state of affairs. The very strict laws governing the use of the public highways in Britain and the consequent use of tests of one kind and another to sort out the winners meant that the Rally hadn't really progressed very far from the pre-war days, an impression heightened by the fact that starts and finish were still located at some of our better-known seaside resorts. If the road section were to have any meaning at all, the organisers had to pray for bad weather conditions to sort out some of the wheat from the chaff.

Now organising a garden fete or a charity cricket match is usually a fairly safe way of ensuring a steady downpour, not to mention the odd spot of thunder and lightning. But when the British climate is asked to produce bad weather to order — as the RAC Rally organisers hoped for in 1958 — then it can let you down just as badly. So the sun shone and the competitors did 30-miles-an-hour around Britain, the only excitement arising when one driver became so bored by it all that she dozed off and went over the edge of a ravine — which fortunately proved to be only twelve feet deep.

The experience was certainly not daunting enough to prevent the lady joining the chorus of discontent at Hastings.

Something had to be done before the 1959 event. And done it was. The date was switched from March to November and although Blackpool was retained as starting-point, the finish was scheduled to be in London for the first time, at the Crystal Palace motor racing circuit to be precise.

The weather responded to the change of date with gusto. Too much so, in fact, bringing all sorts of other problems in its wake. By the time the competitors reached Scotland, snow and ice had the country in its grip. And nowhere was it worse than on the notorious Devil's Elbow on the Tomintoul-Braemar road. Year after year, this is a road which seems to be closed by snow more than any other in the United Kingdom. This year was no exception.

Drivers arrived at Tomintoul to find the local police warning that the direct route to Braemar was closed by snow. What to do? Many elected to go across country, missing the next control and picking up the route later. A few – despite the police warning – tried to get through direct – and failed.

Even fewer set off to try and find an alternative route to the next control.

One of them was Gerry Burgess: 'When faced with the unexpected closing of the obvious, but optional, rally route at Tomintoul, there was no doubt in my mind what must be done – get to the Braemar Control somehow – because after 1958, the RAC Rally could not be won if a control was missed. Our snap decision paid off as it proved but I shall never understand why there should have been so few who tried to do the same.'

Burgess and his co-driver, Croft-Pearson, had of course studied their regulations very carefully, something which is a vital necessity for success in any Rally. What's more when the crunch came, they remained cool, decided on a course of action, and won through.

Others faced with exactly the same problem either panicked or gave up in despair. And it later became quite obvious that some of them at least had not been so careful as Burgess and Croft-Pearson in doing their homework before the Rally began.

Battling through the blizzards, there must have been quite a few competitors who ruefully reflected on their grumbles of the year before.

Back in London, officials were feeling pretty happy about events. Without doubt this had been a tough rally and as the surviving cars trickled into Crystal Palace, mostly dirty and sometimes battered, it seemed a satisfactory state of affairs all round.

Conditions at the Palace were rather primitive in those days and, for

example, instead of the purpose-built and efficient Press Office block which came later, there was an old London double-decker bus used for this purpose. It was Saturday afternoon and so most of the bus's occupants were from evening newspapers and naturally anxious to get the results as quickly as possible, a winter Saturday always posing problems with football dominating the scene. The results came through. Bill Paulson, of the London *Evening News,* and Bob Walling, of the London *Evening Standard,* grabbed the phones and put their copy through − outright winner, Gerry Burgess in a Ford Zephyr; ladies' winner, Anne Hall in a Ford Anglia.

Ten minutes later, the lads were reaching for the phones again. The German team manager had protested against Burgess being declared the winner. That snow-blocked Highland pass had been decisive and the German, on behalf of his driver, Wolfgang Levy, wanted the stage scrubbed out on the basis that no clear-cut instructions had been given to competitors on whether or not to attempt the laid-down route or make a detour.

So the Press Corps sat shivering in that old bus as the gloom of a November afternoon deepened and some of those chill winds from the North infiltrated over the Cockney landscape.

The Stewards of the Rally rejected the protest.

The Press reached for the phones again. Burgess and his co-driver, S. Croft-Pearson, were declared the winners for the second time.

Five minutes later it was all back in the melting-pot. The Germans had exercised their right to appeal against the decision of the Rally Stewards and go over their heads to the Stewards of the RAC, rather in the way that a decision taken at a horse-race meeting may go on appeal to the Stewards of the Jockey Club.

Fortunately, or so we thought from a press point of view, there were enough of the RAC Stewards present, headed by Chairman, Wilfrid Andrews, for them to sit there and then.

And they rejected the German appeal.

That wrapped it up as far as we were concerned. Again eager hands clasped clammy phones and bad-tempered subs were assured that this really was the final decision. All the press boys then departed leaving Pat Gregory and myself to gather up our bits and pieces before rushing back to London and hurriedly changing in time for the prize-giving at the Talk of the Town.

A former newspaperman, Steve Morris, now a PRO consultant, dropped in for a chat and while he was standing there, someone came rushing over from the marquee which served as Rally HQ. He was carrying bombshell tidings.

Normally speaking, the decision of the RAC Stewards would have been **91** final. Providing those protesting were British. But foreign entrants had the right to appeal to 'the House of Lords' as it were, by raising the matter with the FIA, the international controlling body, through their own National Automobile Club, in this case the German Club. And that is just what they did.

The prize-giving had to be cancelled. But it was too late to cancel the prize-giving function and that was to go on.

But in that old double-decker bus we had other problems. All the newspapers and agencies would declare Burgess the winner unless we did something about it. So with the cheerful aid of Steve Morris, Pat and I got to work. Some of the recipients of our news were disbelieving, some sore and most others grateful. So when we had covered every one we could think of, it was helter-skelter back to London, into the old tuxedos with barely a lick and a polish, hello to anxious wives and off in a fast-trotting hansom to the Talk of the Town.

Where, in the case of this writer, insult was added to injury. With the first drink of the day in hand, a page came up with the message that the News Editor of a Sunday paper was on the phone. Hurrying to take the call, glass still in hand, I slipped, fell and cut my hand badly as the glass shattered. Nor was my frame of mind improved by hearing a voice say, 'I suppose he's had a few.'

A prize-giving without prizes is a bit of a non-event but most people had made up their minds to have a good time in spite of everything and food, wine, cabaret and bands soon dispelled the gloom.

But it was to be many weary weeks before the matter was finally settled. Then the FIA announced their decision. They too had rejected the German protests and Burgess, once and for all, was the winner.

We arranged a special prize-giving ceremony at the Connaught Rooms with Earl Howe to hand over the awards. If we thought our troubles were over we were mistaken. It was a cold wet night with a heavy drizzle of rain sliming the pavements.

The television film crews were just setting up their equipment when a messenger burst in: 'Get to Clarence House as quickly as you can. Princess Margaret's got engaged to a feller named Jones.' My face must have registered the despair I felt. 'Don't worry,' said one of the cameramen, 'if you can get the prize-giving started right away, we'll do the job here first.' 'Besides,' said the other, 'it's raining and the police outside Clarence House won't be serving such good whisky.'

That must have been the quickest prize-giving in history but at least it got into the news bulletins and on the movie house circuits in face of some pretty tough opposition. After all, it isn't every day that a Royal Princess gets engaged to 'a feller named Jones'.

Gerry Burgess, a former cycling champion, had waited a long time for his reward and I think it's probably fair to say that, at the time, Gerry felt a little bitter about the whole sorry process which had had to be gone through before justice was done.

Today a successful manufacturer, he still has the urge for competition and in 1969, set some sort of Continental record in a furniture van in order to get an export consignment to a customer when more conventional methods of transport could not meet the deadline.

Anne Hall, who was to win the Ladies Award again the following year, stayed at the top of the rally tree for some time, although in the RAC, she eventually had to give way to a string of successes by Pat Moss.

The 1959 Rally was unique in the manner of its protests but even the most enthusiastic adherent of rallying has to face the fact that protests are frequent at the end of events. Supporters of other sports sometimes turn their noses up at this and say something like, 'They can't be very good sportsmen.'

This is pretty much nonsense. That great Swedish driver, Erik Carlsson, who won the RAC three years on the trot, is generally regarded as a good sport and a fine fellow. But after his victories in 1960, 1961 and 1962, he was placed third in 1963 – and immediately lodged a protest. Some folk thought this bad sportsmanship but, in fact, Carlsson had no choice. He was driving for Saab who, like many other manufacturers, had invested a great deal of time and money in their entries for the Rally. If they thought they had been unjustly treated, they had every right to protest.

There are two basic reasons for protests in an international rally. One is that at this level, car and accessory manufacturers and the big oil companies, are backing the sport for advertising, publicity and prestige purposes. They want to win. And within the framework of the rules, they do everything possible to win.

The second reason – and this applies equally to the works teams and private entrants – is that no matter how efficient the rally organisation, the marking is detailed and complex and mistakes can be and are made. So many hundreds of officials are required to run a big event that it is inevitable that now and again one makes a mistake which, unless spotted, can throw all the results awry.

The RAC has been fortunate through the years in having a most efficient **93**

The great Erik Carlsson in contemplative mood

Below *Carlsson checks up on his engine before his unsuccessful bid in 1963 to win the Rally for the fourth time*

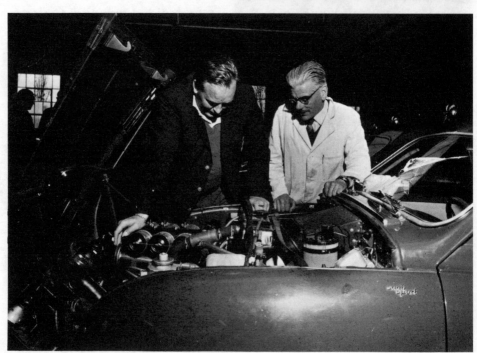

Mrs. H.B. Ehringe and Miss A.L. Lindquist (SAAB) chase by M.A. Costello and G. Cooper (Sunbeam Rapier) on the 1963 RAC

A worse-for-wear SAAB turns off the road on to Forestry Commission land during the 1963 event

95

Results Team, headed for a long, long time by 'Scoop' Russell, of whom more anon. But even their gimlet eyes are not psychic and they must take most marks and timings at face value, unless the difference between one competitor and the rest is so glaring that it obviously needs query. So slight errors may not be spotted until all the details are published at the finish and individual competitors have the opportunity of checking them. That's why time is always allowed for protests afterwards.

Such protests are considered by the Stewards of the Rally and here again the RAC has been fortunate in having men available with the ability to cut right to the heart of a problem. One thinks of people like Wilfrid Andrews; the late John Gott, Chief Constable of Northants and Vice-Chairman of the RAC Competitions Committee, who possessed the tremendous asset of having been an outstanding international rallyist himself; the Marquess of Camden, Chairman of the Comps Committee; and overseas Stewards like Piet Nortier, from Holland; Claude Fin, one of the organisers of the famed Monte Carlo Rally; and Jim Gunn, for many years organiser of the Shell 4000 Rally in Canada.

With men like these, competitors are assured of a fair and full hearing and an objective and impartial decision.

The Stewards have often got the most thankless job of anyone connected with a rally. Sometimes the protests last through most of the night and a Steward must resign himself to loss of sleep and meals. For instance, at the conclusion of the 1968 RAC, the *Sun* newspaper sponsoring the event, laid on a most delightful lunch with Hugh Cudlipp, Chairman of the International Publishing Corporation, amongst those present. But there were a number of empty chairs. The Stewards were still hearing protests. These protests, in fact, did not concern the major awards but the Stewards ensure that justice is done to the lowliest competitors as well as the stars.

Some of the *Sun* executives were worried that their chief, attending a Rally function for the first time, might be put out by this atmosphere of organised chaos. They need not have worried.

'Take no notice of me,' said Hugh Cudlipp, 'it's no use running an event like this and not getting the results right.'

The disputed 1959 Rally ended a decade in which the event had had many ups and downs. The next ten years were to be amongst the best in the Rally's history when, for the first time, competitors in this Cinderella sport would at last make some impression on the public consciousness. Many drivers of many nationalities would compete in the RAC but it was the Scandinavians, following in the successful wake of Erik Carlsson and happily driving in conditions akin to their home land, who would dominate.

Carlsson, the trail-blazer, is a giant of a man, around 6ft. 4in. and weighing seventeen stone and the rest. Which adds to sheer effrontery of his nickname for wife Pat Moss whilst she was expecting their first-born – 'Fatty'. Nor is Erik's shadow likely to grow less. Show-jumping ace, Alan Oliver, whose personal choice in cars is for a Saab, tells me that if feeling hungry you can do no better than wangle an invitation to dinner at the Moss-Carlsson table.

Born at Trollhattan, Sweden, on March 5th, 1929, Carlsson began his motor sport career, as have so many, on motorcycles then made his first rally appearance as a co-driver in the Swedish Rally to the Midnight Sun in 1953. He drove a Saab for the first time the following year then joined the works as a full-time test driver in 1957.

There's hardly a major rally he has not won: The Thousand Lakes, the Midnight Sun, German, the Greek Acropolis, the Italian Rally of the Flowers, etc. But his greatest triumphs have been reserved for the RAC and the Monte – the first man to win the RAC two years on the trot (and he won it again a third time for good measure) and another record-breaking feat in winning the Monte in successive years – 1962 and 1963.

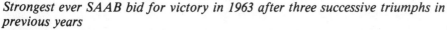

Strongest ever SAAB bid for victory in 1963 after three successive triumphs in previous years

THE STORY OF THE RAC INTERNATIONAL RALLY

For good measure Erik has been Swedish champion on ice and in standard cars and during his military service earned the title of 'Sweden's best soldier'.

He is a very, very tough competitor and European champion, Eugen Bohringer, labelled him 'the blond devil' after the German's struggle with him in the 1962 Monte.

The Crown Prince who succeeded to the Carlsson throne, at least as far as the RAC Rally was concerned, is another Swede, Tom Trana. He comes from Kristinehamm in Central Sweden and, oddly enough, made his first appearance in Britain not in a Rally but in the Brands Hatch 6-Hour Saloon Car Race where, driving with another leading rallyist, Carl-Magnus Skogh, he finished fourth overall. That year he won the RAC, his first major international victory and emulated Carlsson by winning again the following year. Tragedy prevented his bid to equal Carlsson's hat-trick, however. Competing in the Gulf London Rally, Trana's car was in collision with a non-competing car and his co-driver was killed. It was to be a couple of years before Trana made a welcome re-appearance in the RAC.

Not that the Swedes were to have it all their own way in the sixties. Prominent in the Rally story are three Finns, Aaltonen, Makinen and Lampinen, of whom it is arguable that Aaltonen was a shade the best at his peak. His is the story of the understudy who leaped to fame overnight, his big chance coming when he was brought in late as co-driver to Bohringer, leader of the German Mercedes team, just before the 1961 Polish Rally.

His brilliant driving in that event heralded the arrival of a new rally super-star. He had a bit of a reputation as a car-wrecker in his early days and his connection with the Mercedes team was severed after one such occurrence. BMC stepped in smartly and consequently garnered dividends with a host of major wins, coupled with a European Championship for Rauno. Rauno, a married man, who back home in Turku, Finland, sells motor boats, cars, motorbikes and aeroplanes 'anything that goes fast' – has another claim to fame. Sister Marjatta, who was to make a brief appearance in the 1965 RAC, was quite the most glamorous newcomer of the rallying year and Rauno suddenly developed a host of new friends.

Success was to elude Makinen on many an occasion in the RAC although times without number he was the 'pacemaker'. His rallying career went side by side by side with the spectacular sixties of the RAC, Timo himself taking part in his first rally in 1960 and scoring his first international win in the Tulip. His biggest success was to come in the 1965 Monte when, with Paul Easter as co-driver, he chalked up an outright win. And then in the seventies he achieved the success in the RAC which he had fought for so long. Timo comes from Helsinki where he sells cars. Customers must find their test drives most exhilarating with the 'Flying Finn'.

Lampinen, younger than his two countrymen, has triumphed over grave disability to get to the top of the rally tree. An infantile paralysis victim, he was a semi-invalid for several years but fought back and took part in his first rally in 1961 − five days after obtaining a driving licence.

Although the Swedes and Finns were to take the major honours in the RAC during the next ten years, it must not be thought that home drivers gave up without a struggle. At least two, Paddy Hopkirk and Vic Elford, were good enough to win the Monte and Hopkirk probably has the distinction of being the only rally driver ever heard of by a majority of the great British public until the advent of Roger Clark.

Piano-playing Paddy, who studied engineering at Trinity College, Dublin, now runs a successful motor accessory business and in 1969 became a 'proud poppa' for the first time. He belied his 'playboy' image by training hard for international rallies and adopted as his creed 'If you make a mistake don't give up − press on to the finish.'

He made his RAC debut in 1956, driving a Standard Ten, and after that was invariably up with the leaders year after year. Apart from his wins in the Monte, the Austrian Alpine and the Tour de France, Paddy has an unparalleled record of success in his native Circuit of Ireland and has also done well on the race circuit with class wins at Le Mans and Spa, for example. But rallying was his first and major love.

Elford, too, driving mainly for Ford and latterly for Porsche, was also a very versatile driver, extremely successful in touring car racing and a regular on the Grand Prix circuit. Vic shared many rally drives in the first part of the sixties with another top British driver, David Seigle-Morris, then in later years his regular partner became David Stone. Several times in the RAC, victory was to seem within Vic's grasp but always came disappointment. In the Monte too it was much the same story. In 1967, Vic and David Stone led nearly all the way then two hours from the finish were caught in a snowstorm without snow tyres. The following year − 1968 − made up for it. They finished the first mountain circuit just 14 seconds behind Larousse in an Alpine and set out on the final 12-hour circuit determined to make up for the disappointment of the previous year. Then 'big match' nerves overcame Vic and they began to drop further behind. After two 'strung up' tests, David decided it was time to deliver a 'quieten down' talk to his driver. The pyschology worked. On the third stage, Vic was almost a minute faster than

Erik Carlsson and Stuart Turner rise through the floorboards at London's Talk of the Town in their RAC-winning SAAB

101

Larousse and they took the lead by 20 seconds. Larousse crashed on the next test and that was that.

If Britain's No. 1 drivers have had singularly little luck in winning their own rally at least home-bred co-drivers have shared the fruits of victory. Such a one is Tony Ambrose, another former engineering student, who was a member of Lyndon Sims' RAC-winning crew as far back as 1956. He was with Makinen when that worthy won the Tulip in 1964 and with Aaltonen the same year in the winning car in the Spa-Sofia-Liège, when they finished 28 minutes ahead of Erik Carlsson. The following year he shared Aaltonen's European Championship triumph, retired briefly from the fray in 1966, then came back to further successes. In 1969, he was appointed to the organisational staff of the World Cup Rally.

Another Swede with a good record in the RAC is Ove Andersson, from Uppsala, who learned to drive on the family farm when he was only nine. Many ambitious youngsters have saved hard to buy themselves a car but Ove's method must take the biscuit. He volunteered for duty with the United Nations along the Gaza strip – and duly saved the required £500 for a second-hand Saab. Ove's everyday driving is over rough roads and in winter it takes at least a foot of snow before people leave their cars in the garage. It is this sort of motoring, says Ove, which gives Swedish drivers an inbuilt advantage when it comes to rallying. But he destroys one belief – that all Scandinavians like Sauna baths. 'Not me,' says Ove, 'I collapsed in one when I was twelve years old because it was too hot and I've never liked them since.'

Top British star, Roger Clark, learned to drive even earlier than his oft-time Ford team-mate, Andersson. He was only eight when he used to perform on a two-acre field behind the family garage at Narborough (Leics). Most of his rallying career has been spent with the same co-driver, Jim Porter, and the breakthrough for the partnership came in 1964 with wins in the Scottish, Welsh and Gulf London rallies.

On the subject of what makes a rally driver, Roger says, 'I think you are born with the talent and that combines with a developed sense of co-ordination. My reactions are not that quick but I probably have a better sense of balance than a lot of others. Driving isn't hard work to me, by that I mean I don't have to think about what I'm doing all the time.'

Another product of the sixties is Scottish Andrew Cowan, who soared to fame as outright winner of the London to Sydney Marathon. A farmer from the same area of Berwickshire as the great Jim Clark, Cowan's first big win was to come in the Scottish Rally of 1962. Later he was signed up for the

Above Left *Andrew Cowan, the driver from the Borders, who was to make his name in the world long-distance rallies*

Above *Paddy Hopkirk, who burst upon the rally scene in the early sixties, seen in the 1969 RAC when he and Tony Nash drove for Triumph*

Left *Ove Anderson, of Sweden, was another star driver who came on the RAC scene in the Hopkirk-Cowan-Elford era*

103

Top left *Tony Ambrose, a leading navigator who became a world cup organiser*

Top right *Gunnar Palm, RAC-winning navigator who later became a key man in Ford of Sweden's competitions set-up*

Right *Wisecracking Tony Fall, from Bradford, was a BMC works driver and subsequently became the boss man of Dealer Team Opel*

Tom Trana, the Swede who succeeded to Erik Carlsson's mantle

Below *The Morley brothers, top international rallyists with the BMC works team — and the last to wear sports jackets and trousers*

Rootes team and then when they bowed out of competition motoring, he switched to British Leyland.

Britain enjoyed international victories from the likes of Clark and Cowan and from Bradford's Tony Fall, whose international career can really have been said to get in stride with a class win in the 1964 RAC. His other successes have included the rare distinction of winning the Polish Rally.

Roy Fidler, from Stockport, was a British driver often under-rated whereas anyone studying the RAC Rally results over the years can note some very fine performances from him. Certainly he was good enough to become No. 1 driver in the Triumph works team but a crash during the Alpine Rally in which Roy suffered a broken leg was a major setback. Nevertheless, when Datsuns made their successful Rally debut in the 1969 RAC, there was Roy sharing the wheel in the winning team with John Sprinzel, another veteran of the rally wars.

There was a well-known motor sport team known as 'Ecurie Cod Fillet' and Roy was 'King Cod'. This stems from the fact that he was managing-director of a firm of wholesale, retail and fried fish merchants. He held one strong view on rallying – all breakfast halts should serve fish.

Successful co-drivers on the RAC could hardly be mentioned without including the name of Gunnar Palm, whose dark good looks make him the pin-up boy of many of the girls. A former cycle speedway racer and ice hockey player, Gunnar started rallying in 1957. 'Of course, I wanted first to be a driver but I could never afford to buy my own car.' So instead he concentrated on becoming one of the best No. 2's in the business. In 1963, he won the Monte with Erik Carlsson and that same year, as he puts it, 'I started getting paid for my hobby.' In 1966 he joined the Ford works team and spent eight or nine months of the year on rallies. He loves skiing, hopes the mini-skirt fashion lasts for ever, and believes there is no short cut to the top of the rally tree, 'the only way is to go out and practice like hell'. He is now a top man for Ford in Sweden.

Another accomplished co-driver is Henry Liddon, who enjoyed many successes with the BMC team in the sixties. Like Palm, he decided to concentrate on being a top-class navigator after a short-lived career as a driver which began in 1952. He has been in the winning car on the Tour de France, the Monte (twice), the Tulip and Czech rallies and the Circuit of Ireland. Married, with two daughters, he met his wife appropriately enough in a car showroom.

In the late sixties, yet another Finn appeared on the scene – Hannu

Mikkola, from Helsinki. He didn't start rallying in earnest until 1966 but was

Left *The engine compartment of the rally version of the SAAB 96 — two twin Webers with filters and inlet manifold taking most of the space. The block is standard with a single cam and original push-rods*

Below *A familiar sight in the early sixties — a SAAB on one of the special stages*

good enough to be signed up by the Swedish Volvo team and in 1967 got a works drive for Lancia in the Monte. 'My style,' he says, 'is a lot of going sideways.' He goes on to explain, that when he started rallying in Finland, 'We didn't have things like pace notes, so we didn't know which way the road was going after a hump, so it became necessary to get the car sideways to help you round the corner!'

Harry 'Sputnik' Kallstrom, is the son of another Swedish champion, Gunnar. As soon as Harry was old enough to get a driving licence, he asked Gunnar for the loan of his old competition car. Gunnar agreed, saying 'If you beat me with that old car, I'll give up motor sport for the rest of my life.' So father drove his new car in the next rally and finished fourth − Harry drove the old one in this, his very first rally − and finished third.

Gunnar's subsequent remarks have not been recorded for posterity. Despite a bad crash in 1961 when he sailed fifty feet through the air, Harry came back to win the European Championship in 1969.

Above *Paddy Hopkirk, popular Irishman and one of the few home rally stars to become a household name*

Left *A rare sight on the RAC: during the Carlsson era, the Rally once culminated in races in the rain at Brands Hatch. Despite the abundance of Mini's, the overall winner was Carlsson, whose SAAB can be seen on the extreme right of the front row*

109

THE STORY OF THE RAC INTERNATIONAL RALLY

A British driver whom the Scandinavians could not afford to ignore during the RAC Rallies of the sixties was Tiny Lewis, a 6ft. 3in. garage proprietor from Bristol, who led the Rootes team year after year. A good-humoured, friendly man, one of Tiny's best performances came in the 1965 Tulip Rally, in which he was second. There were blizzards in the Jura Mountains and at one stage snow was falling at the rate of a foot an hour. Only 47 out of 157 starters reached Noordwijk within the time limit.

A driver who never quite lived up to his reputation as far as the RAC Rally was concerned was Gunnar Andersson, boss of Volvo's competition activities. European Champion in 1958, the first Swede to hold the title, things were not to go too well with him on the RAC and a sixth place was the best that Britain was to see of him. Illness kept him away one year and, all in all, the records do not do justice to a man whose achievements include outright wins on the Midnight Sun, Adriatic and German rallies and victory in the Mille Miglia and Gran Premio Argentina.

Two of the most reliable of British drivers in the sixties were to be David Siegle-Morris and John Sprinzel. Sprinzel, motor engineer-cum-journalist, is a well-known figure wherever rallyists foregather.

Typical of the man is that he began at the sport right at the top — by co-driving in the 1955 RAC. He was to justify that confidence in later years by finishing as high as second place in the individual stàndings and by being a member of a winning manufacturers team. Believes in training — on oysters, steaks and milk and as proof of his keenness instances that he and wife Pamela 'were married on November 13, 1964 — at the end of the road section of the RAC Rally. Our rally car took us to the ceremony.'

Siegle-Morris, an architect by profession, must have some claim to being one of the best team men in the business. A works driver for Standard-Triumph, BMC and Ford in turn, he had class and team wins in more than one RAC, not to mention the Alpine, Tulip and Monte Carlo Rallies. With Vic Elford he scored an outright win in the Tour de France and was to have shared the wheel with Graham Hill in the ill-fated 1967 RAC Rally.

The ranks of private entrants in the sixties were to include at least three men — Jack Tordoff, Jim Bullough and John Bloxham — who would demonstrate exceedingly well that rallying could be combined with a successful business career. To RAC national rally championships, all three could add some highly successful performances in 'the big one' itself.

These then are some of the men who as the acrimony of 1959 faded were about to set their imprint on the RAC Rallies of the sixties.

Down in the Forest

CAME THE revolution. Being a British revolution it was a quiet one. The 1959 Rally which had included a few stages over private land had reinforced the opinion gained when Eppynt had been included some years previously: that if international rallying was to continue in the British Isles, all the competitive sections must be on private property, leaving the public highway merely as a link between these special stages.

With the co-operation of the Forestry Commission, the War Office and some private land-owners, this was the format agreed upon for 1960.

Thus the 1960 RAC to all intents and purposes began the great years of the Rally when it established a world-wide reputation.

The date was fixed in the international calendar for November. The route was to cover 2,064 miles from the start at Blackpool to the finish at Brands Hatch, the race circuit just outside London, the major part of the route being over Scottish roads and remote tracks never used before in the rally. The organising committee did, however, hedge their bets. Tests at hill-climbs and race circuits were still included and the event was to culminate in a series of 5-lap races at Brands Hatch.

There was to be a ramp start à la the famous Italian road race, the Mille Miglia, and noise-meters were to be used to check that the cars did not create a nuisance. A brochure was printed in four languages to attract overseas competitors and this, coupled with the fact that the Rally was the deciding event in the 1960 European Championship would, it was hoped, bring about an outstanding entry.

And that it did. No less than 180 cars were entered representing 15 British manufacturers and 9 Continental, a 27 per cent improvement on 1959.

Amongst the foreigners were Walter Schock and Rolf Moll (Mercedes) and Rene Trautmann (Citroën) who were the leading contenders for the Championship. Under the then scoring system, the Germans had to finish in the first three to take the title if Trautmann kept going but the Frenchman needed an outright win.

To add to the interest, there was also an international struggle for the Women's Championship between Britain's Pat Moss and Ann Wisdom, driving an Austin Healey Sprite and Sweden's Ewy Rosqvist and her sister Anita Borg, in a Volvo. The British girls were ahead but if the Swedes could repeat their Coupe des Dames victory in the recent German Rally they would tie for the championship.

The most popular category of cars entered was for medium tourers (41) followed by what might be termed the smaller family-type saloons (33). There were 24 cars apiece in the two categories for sports cars but the main focus of interest was the numerically smallest class which embraced the larger type of saloon. The ten entries in this section included the works Mercedes and Citroëns who were expected to put up a great battle. In the final outcome, the excitement was to come from other sources.

But first, the organisers had a little surprise for the competitors up their sleeves and just a few hours before the 'off' it was announced that an additional test was to be included – a skid-pan at Wolvey, near Leicester.

There was another surprise too for those familiar with their motor sport. The Competition Number 13 is usually avoided for reasons of superstition but this time there was a No. 13, on the Aston Martin driven by D.P. Baker, of Wolverhampton. Mr Baker seemed remarkably unperturbed at the prospect.

First car away from the Blackpool start was the Austin-Healey of the Morley brothers, Donald and Erle, and behind them came great rallying names like Sydney Allard, Ronnie Adams, John Sprinzel, Gerry Burgess, the 1959 winner, Eric Jackson, Peter Bolton and Anne Hall.

From the Lancashire seaside resort, the route lay through the Pennines to Brough, over the Scottish border to Charterhall, near Edinburgh and then a breakfast halt at Peebles. From there to the Rest And Be Thankful hill-climb and 180 miles to the overnight halt at Inverness. Then a 300 mile figure of eight which incorporated the tough forest stages and back to Inverness for breakfast. Where rest assured, porridge really does taste better with a liberal addition of salt. Then the long haul to London, with a few diversions for race circuits – and skid pans – en route.

Coming events do cast their shadows before them and the 1960 Rally was to bring a foot-and-mouth scare, the appalling livestock disease which was to bring about the complete cancellation of the 1967 event. What, you may ask, has a farming disease to do with a motoring rally? In short, the rally cars could be the innocent means of transporting the disease from one area to another. This suspected outbreak was in Scotland and RAC patrols worked all through the night to re-locate signs on roads in the Charterhall and Peebles districts. The tests which were to have taken place on the Charterhall racing circuit early on the Tuesday morning were cancelled.

'If the situation does not improve, we may even have the spectacle of the rally cars being disinfected,' said organising secretary Jack Kemsley. (In fact, arrangements did have to be made for this to be done when the cars reached Mallory Park later in the rally).

Sensation piled upon sensation. The rain poured down for the start and then came reports that part of the route near Fort Augustus, in Scotland, was flooded. More re-routing. The scrutineers rejected twelve cars as having unsuitable windscreens and new ones had to be hurriedly fitted.

Eventually 172 cars left Blackpool. Soon the retirements started, amongst the early ones being the redoubtable Mr Baker who found that '13' was unlucky after all. Then disaster overcame Trautmann and ended the Frenchman's admittedly slim hopes of taking the European Championship. To everyone's astonishment, the two surviving Mercedes, including that driven by the new champions, Schock and Moll, withdrew from the Rally, apparently since their objective of securing the title had been achieved. Following on the previous year's debacle which had arisen out of German protests, the Mercedes team were hardly the most popular outfit around Rally circles.

After all these early shenanigans, the survivors were left to get on with the serious business of rallying and by the half-way stage, a Swedish driver who was to become very, very famous indeed, Erik Carlsson (Saab) was the only competitor with a clean sheet. As the weary crews swung southward towards Brands Hatch, it became a question as to whether or not one of four British entries, the Morleys (Austin-Healey), Tiny Lewis (Triumph), Johnny Wallwork (Volvo) or John Sprinzel (Austin-Healey) could catch the galloping Swede.

There was also a tense three-cornered battle going on between Anne Hall (Ford), Ewy Rosqvist (Volvo) and Pat Moss (Austin-Healey) to decide the Ladies Championship.

And at Brands Hatch, even more primitive than today, it rained and rained and rained and everywhere was mud. That 'Beau Brummel' of *113*

Overnight halt in Blackpool: the Volkswagen 1500 of Larsson and Neilson heads off in front of an Anglia

motoring journalists, Tommy Wisdom, screwed his monocle firmly into his eye, settled into a leather armchair in RAC headquarters at Pall Mall and kept in touch with Brands Hatch by telephone. He had the right idea.

The races were a bit of an anti-climax. Conditions were bad and some of the cars were worse. Not only were the drivers weary but so were the engines. Just the same, some drivers, Anne Hall amongst them, signed-off with a flourish and gave those hardy spectators who had braved the elements something to shout about.

When it was all sorted out, Carlsson had triumphed although Sprinzel and the Morley brothers were still breathing hard down his neck at the finish. The works Austin-Healeys swept aside all opposition for the Manufacturers Team Award, the Morley brothers, Pete Riley and Ronnie Adams, being 64 points clear of the second team, Ford. And Anne Hall, with one of the finest performances ever put up by a woman in the RAC had a decisive victory over Pat Moss and Ewy Rosqvist.

The honours, however, were Carlsson's and one can do no better than quote *Motoring News*: 'He laid low a myth; the myth that he is an over-exuberant driver prone to crash his car. "On the roof" Carlsson they have been calling him but it was "On the road" that he proved himself last week.'

Far from crashing, the only damage sustained by the Carlsson Saab occurred after the Rally. Parked outside London's Talk of the Town for the prize-giving, the twin fog-lamps and front panels of the Saab were broken when a wayward London motorist reversed into it.

Incidentally, Carlsson's co-driver was Stuart Turner, then Sports Editor of *Motoring News* but later to become the most famous team manager in the rally world as the Minis and Healeys of the British Motor Corporation swept to victory after victory. Stuart left rallying for a time to join the publicity staff of Castrol but he couldn't keep away and bobbed up again as competitions manager of Ford, where he was to enjoy further success.

When Carlsson and Turner, complete with Saab, rose through the floorboards at the Talk of the Town they were given a fantastic reception, quite something bearing in mind that the star of the cabaret was the fabulous Eartha Kitt. Eartha too brought the house down – and a blush to the hardened cheek of that great character and motoring journalist, the late Gregor Grant, when she made him the object of attention during one of her songs.

There could be no argument when plans were laid for the 1961 event – the success of the previous year's Rally meant that every effort had to be made to include as many special stages over forestry land as possible. The Forestry Commission made available extensive areas in various parts of the country, permitting over 200 miles, more than ten per cent of the course, to be planned over particularly exacting terrain.

Details of the precise, high-speed routes over about twenty of these special stages were to be kept secret and not divulged to competitors until shortly before the 'off'.

Again the start was to be at Blackpool and via the Pennines to Scotland. After tackling Rest And Be Thankful, there was to be a breakfast halt at Inveraray then on to the overnight halt at Inverness. Winding their way through the Highlands, the crews then had to turn south to another breakfast halt at Scarborough then across the Midlands to the Welsh border, another breakfast halt, and an 'easy' run to the finish at Brighton. Here, habit died hard and various tests were to be undertaken on the promenade – shades of the pre-war rallies.

A big public relations bid was mounted to prevent ill-informed criticism of the event and five thousand leaflets were distributed along the route to local authorities, police and other interested parties to advise them of the time the rally would be passing through their area. The leaflet also explained just what the Rally was all about and what an important part such events

A Ford Cortina on stage in the 1963 RAC

Jorma Lusenius and Mike Wood (Mini Cooper S) on a special stage in Wales

1963 — and one of the heavy Rovers which did surprisingly well in rallies about this time sends the gravel flying as it mounts a steep gradient

Tiny Lewis (Sunbeam Rapier) tackles a War Department stage at Lulworth on his way to a class win in the 1962 RAC

played in our national economy. It was hoped that it would correct any false impressions that the Rally is a road race just because the cars carry competition numbers.

It is extraordinary, that even today, there are still people who cannot or will not understand that a rally like this takes part to all intents and purposes off the public highway and that the normal roads bear no competitive element at all. I remember during one Rally being called to the ATV studios at Elstree to take part in a discussion on the subject chaired by the late Edgar Lustgarten. Analytical legal mind that he had, even Mr Lustgarten had the idea firmly in his mind that the rally cars were racing along the public highways and nothing I could say would dissuade him otherwise. It developed into quite an argument, and, although ATV promptly sent along a cheque, as far as I know the programme has never been screened to this day.

Anyway, for better or worse, the Rally organisers bid to put the general public into the picture was well-received in most quarters and all looked set for a first-class event. There were 161 entries, eight of them women, and the list included most of Europe's leading drivers, including Carlsson, the 1960 winner. Amongst them were the top contenders for the Championship, Bohringer (Mercedes), winner of the Polish Rally; his co-driver, Rauno Aaltonen (mark the name well), winner of the Thousand Lakes; and Hans Walter (Porsche), first in the German Rally. Then there was the 1958 Champion, Gunnar Andersson (Volvo), Britain's Tulip Rally winner, Geoff Mabbs (Triumph) and the farming Morley brothers, Donald and Erle, victors in that year's Alpine. And there was to be a repeat performance of the 1960 three-cornered battle of the fair sexes between the reigning champions, Pat Moss and Ann Wisdom, the Swede, Ewy Rosqvist and Huddersfield's Anne Hall. This time the championship would not depend upon the result since the blonde Swede had already made sure of being the new champion by her performances in the Acropolis, Alpine, Midnight Sun, Polish and German Rallies.

For the first time in the history of the event, competitors were 'seeded' so as to bring the leading competitors into the first batch of cars. This was not only a help to spectators but, more important, reduced the chances of the favourites being baulked by slower drivers. Timing clocks, valued at more than £25,000, were imported from Switzerland, especially for the event, and caused not a little anxiety to RAC officials, one reason being that unless they were returned to Switzerland within 14 days, the organisers faced a bill from the Customs.

118   Jack Kemsley smacked his lips and said, 'This year will really sort the men from the boys. I'm expecting dozens of cars to drop out during the rugged forest sections and the winner will be a real champion.'

An indication of what big business the Rally was becoming was the fact that this 1961 event required the services of 500 officials, 800 temporary RAC signs and some £30,000 of equipment. Drivers were competing for £1,000 cash and a total of 63 trophies. Such figures were to be dwarfed in the years ahead.

In all there were nine non-starters, the best-known being H. Eger (Mercedes). With his co-driver, von Korff at the wheel, it was reported that he had crashed somewhere in France whilst en route to Blackpool.

Those who did start found the early sections easy going since apart from a little rain and some mist patches, the weather was reasonable. Nevertheless, by the time they reached Peebles, only six crews were unpenalised – Carlsson, Pat Moss, the Morley brothers, Peter Harper and two of the German entries, Hans Walter and Eugen Bohringer. Another fancied driver, Ian Walker (Ford) went off the road and was bogged down, losing three hours before he extricated himself.

Any fears Jack had that the Rally would not live up to his forecast evaporated before the crews reached the overnight halt at Inverness. Competitors were agreed on it being the 'toughest ever' event. Three cars were forced out in a triple collision and a further seventeen either retired or failed to arrive at main controls, thus being automatically eliminated. The collision involved the late replacement driver, John Whitmore (Mini), London garage owner and subsequent record-breaker Ken Chambers (Ford) and M.V. Mackie (Sunbeam). No one was hurt but all three cars were too damaged to continue. The other retirements included Peter Bolton and this was a pity for had he finished it would have been a little bit of history for Peter was driving a TVR, the only car manufactured in Blackpool where the Rally started. Others to go included Irish hope Adrian Boyd (Austin-Healey) and one of the official Army team, Colonel Hook, who hit a bridge in his Vauxhall.

At this stage, Carlsson had lost eight marks but was still ahead of the Morleys, Pat Moss, Peter Harper and Paddy Hopkirk. Walter, first to arrive at Inverness and assured of the European Championship, was sixth. His countryman, Eugen Bohringer, was amongst the retirements.

Yet it was two 'unknowns' of the rally world who reluctantly stole the limelight. They were Peter Burch, of Aldershot, and his co-driver, A. Benniman. They broke a half-shaft three miles from Inverness and with grim determination pushed the car the remaining distance to the control. *119*

Then they struggled desperately to repair the car and get back intó the fray during the hour's grace permitted each competitor after the cars were freed from parc ferme. In the same time, the Saab mechanics almost took Carlsson's car to pieces to ensure that a mechanical failure would not rob him of his second win.

Safely negotiating a secret noise check, the 123 survivors found more trouble on the 13-mile long Culbin Forest stage and Mike Sutcliffe (MG) hit a farm gate blown into his path by the high winds. The car was damaged but Mike was able to carry on.

Paddy Hopkirk also had trouble with a farm-gate – 'the worst experience of my rallying life'.

A five-barred gate that should have been open was closed when Paddy arrived at 60 mph. Outcome – gate demolished and a very narrow escape indeed for Paddy and co-driver, J. Scott, as the wooden bars came close to spearing them.

There was no holding Carlsson, however, and as the cars neared the Brighton finish, the big Swede's hold on the lead became impregnable. It was obvious that, barring accidents, the tests at the finish would resolve only a few of the minor placings.

So it proved, the main excitements of the finishing sequence at Brighton being provided in other ways – which properly have their place elsewhere in this book.

The special stages had arrived to stay and none appreciated them more than the Scandinavian drivers who found the conditions 'just like home', an enthusiasm not shared by other foreign drivers to the same extent.

When the 1962 Rally was announced, some 300 miles of Forestry Commission and War Office Land were included. The start was once again to be in Blackpool but the finish was transferred to Bournemouth, scene of the first post-war RAC Rally in 1951. The total distance was around 2,200 miles and competitors would cross 50 counties.

The status now enjoyed by the event was reflected in a star-studded entry which included the current leader in the European Championship, Eugen Bohringer, in a works-entered Mercedes, former champion Gunnar Andersson, driving a Volvo and, naturally, the giant Erik Carlsson bidding to win for Saab for the third unprecedented occasion. The 'Flying Finn', Rauno Aaltonen, was entered in a British works Morris.

The battle was also to be renewed between that redoubtle threesome of Pat Moss, Ewy Rosqvist and Anne Hall, Pat's previous efforts earning her No. 5 seeding overall.

The drama was not long delayed. Soon after leaving the start, the No. 1 seed, Eugen Bohringer, was out after his Mercedes smashed into a tree. The 1958 winner, Peter Harper, found himself in total darkness when a swinging map-light fused his lights – and the Rapier smashed into a pile of rocks which Providence had thoughtfully provided at the side of the road. The Morley brothers went out too and tragedy was narrowly averted. Their Austin-Healey performed a double somersault at more than 90 miles an hour and Pat Moss, travelling hard on her team-mates' heels, barely pulled up in time. Then she and her co-driver, Pauline Mayman, helped to get the boys out. Donald Morley was taken to hospital with a dislocated shoulder and doubtless was thankful to escape so comparatively lightly.

Carlsson was once again going like a bat out of hell and, alas for the hopes of home drivers, two new Swedish menaces had appeared on the scene, Tom Trana and Bengt Soderstrom.

Two thousand miles is a long way to go, however, and British hopes soared when first Trana retired with transmission trouble and then Soderstrom was towed into Blackpool as the result of gearbox failure. Their withdrawal left Paddy Hopkirk (Austin-Healey) in second place, 39 marks adrift from Carlsson, the leader. But the big Swede was not counting his chickens before they were hatched. Asked if he would appear on television on the Friday night, he said, 'Yes – if I manage to reach Bournemouth.'

Pat Moss was lying fifth overall at this point and although certain to be European Ladies Champion she could not be so certain of winning the Ladies Prize in the RAC for here too another Swedish 'menace' had appeared in the trim person of Volvo driver and ice racing champion, Mrs Sylvia Osterberg.

Plenty of drivers were having adventures. Anne Hall and Val Domleo crashed down a banking into a stream but got out and carried on. Timo Makinen's Mini developed a leaking radiator – and he was saved by a Z-car patrol from the Lancashire police who followed him along the road, topping his radiator up from time to time.

One of the RAF entries, a Mini driven by Squadron-Leader R.F. Bowers, was in collision with a deer. The deer died and the Squadron-Leader's lights went out. He got to the next control by following another car's tail-lights.

Even Carlsson was having his troubles. The locating arm for a rear wheel snapped but fortune was on his side. He found a spectator with a Saab and borrowed the missing link, a coincidence that had many people talking at the time.

Things got stickier and considerably slower in the Welsh mountains. The last night brought snow, ice and mud so thick that one stage had to be cancelled. Anne Hall had her second crash and this time the Anglia went down a banking and stuck. Rosemary Smith used a suede jacket to give purchase to the back wheels of her Alpine and later used a hairpin to replace a fuse when her windscreen wipers stopped working. Bill Bengry, No. 1 in the Rover team, completely re-welded a cracked oil casing – and kept himself in the Rally. And, with the rain falling steadily, Pat Moss and Pauline Mayman had to push their car some distance when water drowned the engine.

In unabated wet weather, Carlsson and co-driver David Stone, steamed into Bournemouth with their lead over Hopkirk increased to 60 marks. 'The finest ever,' beamed Carlsson. 'The most exciting ride of my life,' said his breathless co-driver. 'We're getting nearer first place every time,' said a not dis-satisfied Hopkirk.

And the incredible Pat Moss came in third in front of Tiny Lewis (Rapier), Rauno Aaltonen (Mini) and Henry Taylor (Anglia).

British manufacturers were not too disheartened by Saab's remarkable hat-trick. The BMC team of Aaltonen, Logan Morrison and Makinen took the Manufacturers Award, the Standard-Triumphs of Thuner, Sprinzel and Sutcliffe were second and the Rovers of James, Bengry and Cuff third, quite a performance to get these big cars safely around the tricky forest sections.

So it was on to 1963 with the big question: could anyone stop Carlsson's domination of the Rally?

Well, they could and they did. With route again Blackpool to Bournemouth, there was no letting up in the quality of the entries although for once an Englishman earned top seeding, Geoff Mabbs (Austin Cooper S) being allocated the No. 1 spot after his Tulip success.

But the wise ones looked beyond Geoff for the possible successor to Carlsson, to the array of Scandinavians, here again in full force: Aaltonen, Bertil and Bengt Soderstrom, Andersson, Makinen and the sensation of the previous years' rally, Tom Trana, driving this time in a works Volvo.

Not that there was a lack of intriguing possibilities in the rest of the field: Hopkirk again with the BMC team, the Belgian racing driver Lucien Bianchi (Citroën), Pat Moss in a Ford Cortina, Vic Elford and last year's winning co-driver, David Stone, in a works Triumph, and some very brave gentleman – and one lady in what looked like vastly unsuitable machinery for the forests – Peter Harper in a Humber Super Snipe, BBC commentator Raymond Baxter in a Reliant Sabre and Bo Ljungfeldt, Peter Jopp and Denise McLuggage in the giant Ford Falcons.

Carlsson had a jocular excuse ready should he be defeated. Said he, 'This year's rally will be my first as a British resident and holder of a British driving licence. Now that I am married to Pat Moss I live in England – and that has meant the end of driving here on an international Permit. After our wedding I discovered that I would have to take a Ministry of Transport driving test before I was allowed out on the roads of Britain in charge of a motor car. So if I do badly this year I will blame it on learning the British driving technique. I must say I have found the hand signals fascinating but I hope they don't slow me down on the way round Oulton Park.'

As it was, the hand signals didn't slow Carlsson down too much but when the smoke had cleared, he was no higher than third. Trana had justified the promise shown the previous year by tooling his Volvo into first place ahead of a works Volkswagen, driven by Harry Kallstrom and Gunnar Haggbom. It was the first time Kallstrom had ever driven on British roads which made his a particularly fine performance. Kallstrom (pronounced 'Shell-strom') was nicknamed 'Sputnik', not without reason. Hopkirk (fourth), Henry Taylor, Pat Moss and the Morley brothers all finished in the first ten to give some crumbs of consolation to home drivers.

Only George Merwin, Competitions manager for Ford of America, was left ruefully to contemplate his pre-rally fighting words: 'The RAC is an ideal rally for the Falcon. These cars have fantastic acceleration, road holding and brake power and I have high hopes of success'.

The rest is silence.

For some time, the rally organisers had wondered if by always starting and invariably finishing in the provinces, the rally was not attracting the attention it might. In 1964, a gamble was taken when, through the co-operation of the Army, the Duke of York's barracks in the heart of the capital was made available for start and finish and a permanent rally HQ was established at the Kensington Palace Hotel, thus obviating the necessity to switch the main control from point to point throughout the country.

The scheduled route put the mileage up to the highest yet – 2,528 – and took competitors first to the West Country then on through Wales, the Lake District and the Border Country to the only overnight halt at Perth. Then it was back down the east side of the British Isles with a diversion into the uncharted regions of East Anglia, of which more anon. As a little gimmick for the benefit of the competing crews, the route was slightly amended to give them the opportunity of driving over the recently-completed Forth road bridge.

The entry-list looked stronger than ever as a glance at the top twenty **123** indicates: Hopkirk (BMC Cooper), Aaltonen (BMC Cooper), Elford (Ford), Carlsson (Saab), Toivonen (Volkswagen), Osterberg (Volvo), Moss (Saab), Trana (Volvo), Bengt Soderstrom (Ford), Lampinen (Saab), Morley (Austin-Healey), Janssen (Volkswagen), Makinen (Austin-Healey), Skogh (Volvo), Lewis (Hillman), Taylor (Ford), Bertil Soderstrom (Volkswagen) and Seigle-Morris (Ford).

With Carlsson and Trana in the field, it may surprise that Hopkirk was No. 1 but seedings were based on the results of the current year's international events and the Irishman had finally got to his first place by winning the famous Monte Carlo Rally in no uncertain style.

With a Sunday start, the time was settled at an early 7 am so that rally cars would not interfere with Remembrance Day parades and services in London and so scheduled that the cars would be at a halt at 11 am for the two minutes silence.

Nor was this the only unusual matter affecting the route. A few days beforehand came a 'shotgun warning'. Three of the new special stages in East Anglia were on Forestry Commission land near the town of Thetford in Norfolk. Permission to use them had been given by the Commission subject to the agreement of a number of people to whom shooting rights had been granted. About 80 of these folk were contacted and most readily agreed that the rally could proceed but some were adamant in their objections. 'Unless they change their minds,' said Jack Kemsley, 'we'll have to change the route. We don't think drivers would appreciate being peppered by shot-gun pellets.'

Paddy Hopkirk was certainly given a morale-booster at the start when a musical send-off came from Pipers of the London Irish Regiment. To add to the military flavour, the Middlesex Yeomanry, the 44th Parachute Brigade, the Royal Engineers, the WRAC and the RAMC co-operated with radio communications, support vehicles, marshals and so on.

But objections to the Rally were apparently contagious. There was a new conservator on some of the forestry land in Wales and he now spoke up to object to the Rally on the grounds that it would bring too many spectators to his forests.

In all 158 starters left the Duke of York's with the final route ahead of them not yet settled. As they headed into Hampshire fog came down, at least one car was reported out already and bright British hope Henry Taylor (Ford) had been heavily penalised after rolling his car on the first special stage.

Makinen was soon in the lead with Trana, Hopkirk, Aaltonen, Elford, Carlsson and Ljungfeldt (this year more suitably 'dressed' in a Cortina) behind him.

Tiny Lewis lost the windscreen on his Hillman Imp at Porlock and when the cars reached Bristol went to his nearby home for some warmer clothing.

As the cars moved into Wales, Makinen stayed in front of Trana but Kallstrom had climbed up into third place. Hopkirk was breathing down Kallstrom's neck but the sad fact remained that seven of the first ten drivers were Scandinavians at this point.

The Rally has always had great appeal to the Welsh and it was well-demonstrated this year when the head of a school at Taliesin gave his pupils a half-day off to see the cars.

Hereabouts, Makinen 'lost it' and Bengt Soderstrom took over the lead with Trana still second. The two car East German team, in the Rally for the first time, was going steadily determined to finish, a policy also being followed by the team of Rovers entered by the British Army Motoring Association.

The 'biffs' and 'bangs' were about to get 'biffier' and 'bangier' however. The Morleys crashed but limped on. Siegle-Morris spun and was hit by two other cars and Trana and Carlsson bumped in the forests. Icy patches and clumps of fog were making it a very lively rally indeed.

By the time the surviving cars reached Oulton Park visibility was down to 20 yards and the planned speed tests became something of a crawl for many competitors. Even so, Paddy Hopkirk clocked 13 minutes, 8 seconds for the 16.5-mile distance, 42 seconds faster than Harry Kallstrom, overall leader of the Rally at this stage. Mechanics had to get busy on one of the cars — that being driven by travelling Press Officer, Graham Snowdon, who had the worst of an argument with a lorry in the fog.

More fog plus the rugged forest sections continued to extract heavy toll as the cars drove North and it was a weary, be-draggled cavalcade which limped into the breakfast-halt at Turnberry. Henry Taylor had crashed again — this time into a ditch — and Aaltonen too had been off the road. Rosemary Smith and Margaret McKenzie broke down at the start of one of the stages and only the resilient Trana, back in the lead again, seemed confident.

Lewis had more trouble with his Imp and the Standard-Triumph team suffered a blow when their all-Swiss crew, Thuner and Gretener, retired.

Amongst the battered machinery at Turnberry, Pauline Mayman and Val Domleo had an unusual problem. The doors of their MG were jammed and they had to climb out through the windows. Hopkirk arrived balanced precariously on his driving seat, the back of which had collapsed.

Kallstrom and Bjork (Mini Cooper S) on a special stage in Wales during the 1965 rally

But the most unusual mishap of all occurred to another member of the Standard-Triumph team, Terry Hunter, who tried to snatch a brief rest, overslept and left the control thirty minutes late.

Still the fog stubbornly refused to go away and the route had to be changed when police closed the Forth road bridge due to the conditions. Around 50 cars were now reported out of the Rally but most of the leaders were still going strong when the cars eventually reached the overnight halt at Perth.

Carlsson commented, 'I spent 18 minutes in a ditch yesterday and I have been taking the route very respectfully ever since.'

Meanwhile, organisers were discussing whether or not the results at fogbound Oulton Park should stand and also if some of the leaders should be penalised for missing a passage control at Settle (Yorks). It was decided that Oulton results would count and that no competitors would be penalised for the Settle incident which apparently resulted from a rally direction sign being obscured accidentally by the local constabulary.

126

Battered but unbeaten, the crew of this Mini seem surprised to have arrived at the top of a hill

With these mysteries cleared up for the moment, Trana emerged as a clear leader over Aaltonen, Kallstrom, Hopkirk and Elford.

Only 103 cars restarted from Perth and only two 'works' teams — the BMC Minis and Fords — were left to contest the manufacturers award.

Then came disaster for Hopkirk. A news flash came through from Pat Gregory in Perth that Hopkirk was reported to have hit a tree. Hardly had the phone call ended when Perth was completely cut off from the outside world. All telephone communication from the town was stopped by a breakdown and Rally HQ in London had no way of finding out what was happening.

When communication was eventually restored, the news about Hopkirk turned out to be true. Also out were Pauline Mayman, top woman driver in the 1964 Alpine Rally, and Rauno Aaltonen. Trana, one observer reported laconically, is 'still going like a bomb.'

Ninety-odd cars were left and now only one works team — the Fords.

The weather had improved — if rain can be regarded as an improvement over fog and ice. Trana, overall leader, and Pat Moss, front runner of the fair sex, arrived safely at Barnby Moor (Yorks) but 'Sputnik' Kallstrom was reported out with gearbox trouble.

With some of the East Anglian stages cancelled because of the shotgun business, the finish was not far off.

Trana was miles in front but Englishman Vic Elford was in second place, ahead of Timo Makinen. And chasing Erik Carlsson for a class award was a four-year-old Mini, rebuilt by B.I. Stevens, of Headcorn (Kent) at a total cost, including entry fee for the Rally, of £100. Makinen was making a strong bid to overtake Elford and although the latter was later to make a name as a racing driver, the Finn was nearly two minutes faster on the speed tests at the Snetterton circuit.

The leaders all kept going to the finish in London and as the Volvo of Trana entered the Duke of York's Barracks a spray of pink carnations was thrown on to the mud-spattered bonnet. Trana, happy at his second successive win, said 'It was quite the toughest rally I have ever competed in and far harder than any I have experienced in Sweden and on the Continent. I shall be back next year and hope to win again.' His win assured him of the European Championship and Pat Moss, by finishing fourth, won the Ladies title. Makinen's storming finish gave him second place over Elford and the Ford team survived intact, the only Manufacturers team to do so.

The RAC Rally was still a happy hunting ground for the Scandinavians...

In general terms, the switch to a London start and finish had been a success. In questions of detail, there had been a number of hitches, not least the fact that a number of rally cars had been towed away from the vicinity of Rally HQ. And a Grand Prix had nothing on the frantic dash most people had to make to get from HQ in Kensington to the prize-giving at Leicester Square's Talk of the Town.

So for 1965 a move was made out of town – but only as far as the Excelsior Hotel at London Airport, where parking facilities at least were more than ample. To avoid Remembrance Day and with the co-operation of three French rallies, the RAC was put back a week towards the end of November.

Yet again a tense struggle was promised for the European Championship between the French ace, Rene Trautmann, in his Italian 'works' Lancia and Finlands' Rauno Aaltonen, in an Abingdon-entered Mini Cooper. The Munich-Vienna-Budapest Rally was the last but one of the events counting towards the title and Aaltonen with an outright win led Trautmann by 75 points to 61. If, and it was a big 'if', Trautmann could win the RAC, Aaltonen would need to finish second, third, fourth or fifth to take the Championship.

For the British Motor Corporation, the 1965 RAC held a special challenge. They had won six of the twelve Championship rallies so far disputed in the season and of those successes, four victories had been gained by the partnership of Aaltonen and Tony Ambrose. And, above all, they desparately wanted to gain the outright win which had so far eluded them.

In 1959, the Austin-Healey of Tommy Gold and Mike Hughes had finished second. In 1960, it was second place again, another Austin-Healey, but this time driven by John Sprinzel and Dick Bensted-Smith.

Unbelievably, 1961 brought another runners-up spot. The car? Austin-Healey, of course. The drivers – Pat Moss and Ann Wisdom. What odds would a bookmaker have offered against an Austin-Healey being second once more in 1962? Well, it was a fact – this one driven by Paddy Hopkirk and J. Scott.

The pattern changed in 1963 when a Mini-Cooper driven by Paddy Hopkirk and Henry Liddon could not manage better than fourth but 1964 brought things back to normal: an Austin-Healey in second place, with Timo Makinen and Don Barrow as crew.

So BMC at least had special reasons for wanting this to be the big year.

No. 1 seed was Tom Trana, winner for the past two years, followed by Timo Makinen and Vic Elford in the order they had finished the previous year. Saab were once again strongly represented with four works cars, led by   *129* three-time winner Erik Carlsson, and eight privateers.

With the events of 1964 very much in mind, the organisers made arrangements for Special Controls should fog descend, promising extra time allowances for competitors if conditions reached a dangerous pitch. But before the start, two special stages in Scotland had to be cancelled for other reasons, gales and generally adverse weather.

The threatened European Championship battle did not materialise. Trautmann withdrew, thus assuring Aaltonen of the title whatever happened. Ironically, on the Wednesday after the Rally was scheduled to finish, the new champion was due to present himself at Oxford — for a Ministry of Transport driving test. Shades of Erik Carlsson.

It rained and rained and rained but 163 cars went through scrutiny. An Army Land-Rover arrived 'out of time' but after the driver pleaded a breakdown, the vehicle was allowed through. Some unkind soul declared that the soldiers had been tucking into eggs and bacon in a cafe down the road at the time they were supposed to be wrestling with a breakdown but other competitors had cause to bless the 'blind eye' act of the scrutineers because the Army men did valiant work in hauling some of them out of trouble on special stages.

The rain soon brought about a casualty, the first stage — under water — having to be cancelled. But there was a big crowd for the start despite the inclement conditions, some of them doubtless drawn by the attraction of Graham Hill acting as official starter.

Ahead of the crews, lay five days and three nights of continuous driving — and from RAC patrols came ominous reports that six inches of snow lay on some Highland roads.

In contrast, the first stage tackled by the competitors was described as 'a sea of mud' which did not deter the Swedish aces, Bengt Soderstrom and Bo Ljungfeldt, both in Lotus Cortinas, from putting up fast times. But after three stages, a dark horse from Norway, Trono Schea (Ford) was in the lead, eight seconds ahead of the old maestro, Timo Makinen. Schea's success brought heady but temporary happiness to Irish Paddy Thornberry, in those days European Sports Editor of the United Press. Getting the telephone message from HQ that someone named Schea was in the lead, Paddy thought for a few blissful moments that at last there was a rally where the hopes of 'ould Oireland' were not entirely dependent on the skilful driving of one Hopkirk.

His face when he later learned that Schea was Norwegian was quite a

study.

1965 — and a move was made to London's Excelsior Hotel: cars assembled before the start

Already at this early period of time, five cars had retired. Two of them were from the NSU team which was thus speedily eliminated from the struggle amongst manufacturers for team honours.

As the survivors tackled the Welsh mountain roads, the Norwegian and the Finn were still at it hammer and tongs with Britain's brightest hope, Paddy Hopkirk, climbing into third place. Makinen eventually nosed in front as Schea began to slip back and another comparative unknown, 25-year-old Tony Fall from Bradford driving a Mini Cooper, steadily improved his times. Nearing the Oulton Park circuit, it was reported that eighteen of the 163 starters had dropped out, amongst them the veteran Peter Harper (Sunbeam Tiger).

Oulton Park had still to be reached, however, and Makinen lost time when he went off the road. Aaltonen, another of the pacemakers, suffered a puncture and Scottish star, Andrew Cowan, rolled his Imp. The Army team was getting encouragement from the performances of Major Preston whose Rover was making good, if not sensational, progress.

Ooooops....

By Monday afternoon as the 140 survivors headed north through Yorkshire to Scotland, things were looking brighter for British cars than for many a long RAC Rally. Six of the first ten were BMC products. In front was Makinen with his team-mates, Hopkirk and Aaltonen, both in Minis, battling for second and third. Fourth was Carlsson, as usual driving for Saab.

Tough road and weather conditions lay ahead for the drivers during their all-night run to Peebles where one of the forestry stages had already been cancelled due to heavy snow. Meantime, Ljungfeldt retired and Carlsson was reported unhappy with a sick engine, Brian Culcheth (Cortina GT) hit a bridge and went into the river, fortunately without damage to driver and passenger. Worst hard-luck story was that of C. Laurent in one of the little Dutch DAFs. He had four punctures on the trot then broke a wheel. Still he fought on.

Came the dawn... and by midday on Tuesday with the delightful prospect of an overnight halt in Perth looming ahead, only 86 cars were left in the Rally. Finland's Simo Lampinen was out with a blown head gasket and Anne Hall and the Morley brothers had disappeared from the lists. Back in front was Makinen, driving like a demon and nearly five minutes up on Aaltonen and Carlsson. Close behind came Kallstrom and Jerry Larsson (Saab).

Happiness is winning the RAC Rally: Aaltonen and Ambrose make free with the champagne after their 1965 victory in a Mini, the first time a British car had won the European Championship since it was instituted in 1953

First into Perth was the glamorous Rosemary Smith (Hillman Imp). The car was undamaged although Rosemary said she had been off the road three times. Makinen too was an early arrival and was surprised to hear that he was in the lead.

Only seventy-one cars left Perth on the long drive south – one thousand miles of motoring with twenty special stages dotted along the route. Official placings at the overnight halt showed the order to be Makinen, Aaltonen, Carlsson, with Stockport fish merchant Roy Fidler (Triumph 2000), the leading British driver at seventh. Bright sunshine greeted the re-start but it was so bitterly cold that most of the crews had to scrape ice from the windscreens.

First away was the leader, Makinen, his Austin-Healey so battered that the only undented portion appeared to be the roof. In contrast, the Saabs of Erik Carlsson and his wife, Pat Moss, had hardly a blemish.

Makinen kept up his furious pace during the first two special stages after Perth but he was being matched for speed by the Ford works driver, Vic Elford. Cheering note for the drivers was that in Lancashire, the local Civil Defence were combining a special exercise with the Rally and maintaining radio links — meanwhile, gleefully rubbing their hands in anticipation of more bad weather to make the exercise interesting.

The competitors were doing pretty spectacularly without excessive aid from the weather. One went down a fifteen feet drop and escaped unhurt. Spectators helped to pull the car back on to the road and Master Jorma Lusenius continued on his way.

There was still plenty of excitement to come. Reports came in that both Vic Elford and Siegle-Morris had crashed and only 66 cars remained. Jerry Larsson had overtaken Carlsson and Roy Fidler had moved up into fifth place. More drama as they halted for breakfast at Devil's Bridge then headed for the finish. Makinen was in trouble and his fellow countryman, Rauno Aaltonen, had gained 49 seconds lead. Disaster had overtaken Timo on one of the special stages in North Wales where an uphill section was covered in sheet ice. Timo had to push the big Austin-Healey to the finish line and so lost valuable time.

It was the decisive moment of the rally. Aaltonen stayed in front the rest of the way with Makinen having to be content with second place followed by Larsson, Carlsson and Roy Fidler.

Said Rauno, 'I'm delighted to win this very tough event but I feel so sorry for poor old Timo.' Said Timo, 'Oh yes, of course I am a little disappointed but that's rallying. Besides, Rauno deserved to win.'

For Britain's manufacturers — if not British drivers — it was a breakthrough, the first time since the European Championship was instituted in 1953 that it had been won by a British car. Aaltonen added, 'Since I am the first driver ever to win the Rally Championship of Europe with a British car, I am particularly pleased that my first success as Champion should be in a British Rally.'

For British drivers, victory in their own rally remained elusive. Fidler, with an honourable fifth place, and Pat Moss, now married to a Swede and driving a Swedish car to tenth position, was the best they could manage...

Now that a British car was capable of winning an event run in these **134** Scandinavian-type conditions could a British driver follow suit?

... Something stirred

WHATEVER THE intentions of British rally drivers, two men much more famous on the race circuits decided to have a go at the 1966 RAC − Jim Clark and Graham Hill.

Jim confessed that the first time he had ever done 100 mph was in a rally − the 1955 Scottish. The experience was short-lived. Jim recalled, 'The owner of the car called a halt to the proceedings and insisted on doing all the driving himself from then on.' Graham's previous international rally experience had been in the 1964 Monte when he drove an American Ford Falcon. 'It hit a mountain,' was his cheerful description of a brush with a rock-face after his throttle jammed open.

The addition of these two naturally added to the public interest which was reinforced by *Sun* sponsorship and good television coverage − indeed the Graham Hill car, with newspaperman Max Boyd in the co-driver's seat, was the official BBC *Wheelbase* and *Sunday Times* entry.

Four previous winners were in the field − Aaltonen, Trana, Carlsson and Harper − and a strong overseas entry included teams from Renault, Lancia and Saab. BMC, Rootes and Fords were upholding the honour of British manufacturers. Monte victor Paddy Hopkirk was again competing and so was the lanky Tiny Lewis, who once more proposed to contort his tall figure into the tiny Hillman Imp. And there were high hopes for Scottish Rally winner, Roger (no relation to Jim) Clark.

Apart from the works teams there were entries from the Civil Service, the British Army and the Police.

And to round off a star-studded assembly, the world champion racing driver, Jack Brabham, agreed to officiate at the start.

The route which included 63 special stages in its 2,400 miles was on similar lines to previous years but the overnight halt was scheduled for Aviemore.

Roger Clark certainly started with a bang and was fastest over the first special stage but Jim Clark did well to register fifth fastest. Graham Hill was not so happy. He got out of his car and said, 'Crikey, what a caper. Give me a cup of tea.'

The weather was clear and dry as they headed west but just the same Tony Fall and Rauno Aaltonen had arguments with a ditch at Lulworth. Fortunately for both, fifty willing pairs of hands got them out. After four stages, the familiar figure of Makinen was in front with Bengt Soderstrom (Ford) second. Equal third was another Finn, Pauli Toivonen (Renault) with Roger Clark. But Roger was in trouble after hitting a tree and had to retire. By Bristol, it was still Makinen and Soderstrom, with Hakan Lindberg (Renault) third and Harry Kallstrom (BMC Cooper) fourth. Then came Toivonen, Aaltonen and Hopkirk.

In Wales, the biggest crowds ever seen on a British rally waited for the cars. Henry Taylor, former racing driver managing the Ford team, said: 'It's fantastic – I've never seen so many people on a Scandinavian rally where the entire population is crazy about the sport.'

Makinen was still leading from Soderstrom, Kallstrom and Aaltonen but much of the interest was centred on Grand Prix ace, Jim Clark, who was working his way steadily up the field and posing a real threat to the leaders. Despite a puncture which resulted in him driving nearly three miles on a flat tyre, he kept going saying, 'I'm just getting the hang of this business.'

At Oulton Park, nearly 10,000 spectators awaited the cars but they could not be allowed into the circuit for a closer look. Commented Oulton Park chief, Rex Foster: 'We do not having planning permission for Sunday activities and even the drivers and mechanics have had to be invited as our guests.'

By the time the cars crossed the Scottish border nearly fifty cars had retired, amongst them the Mini-Cooper of Graham Hill which went out at Grisedale, near Carlisle. Hill was 39th at the time.

Jim Clark, on the other hand, was giving his Scottish countrymen something to shout about, clocking fantastically fast times in his native forests to move up the leader board to seventh position. Another Scot, Andrew Cowan, in a works Imp, was also going well on his home ground and had moved up to twelfth overall.

Clark kept it up and by the time the overnight halt at Aviemore was reached he was in sixth place and had well earned the title 'King of the Forests'. 'I'm getting more confident all the time and reading the signs quicker and better. My only worry is that I might get too confident.'

Makinen was now some six minutes in front of Soderstrom but it would have been a rash man who would have bet on a victory for the Finn. So often before had he led only to meet disaster in the latter stages.

Next morning competitors found that although they had been tucked in bed all night, some positions had changed. What had happened was this: on the Twiglees special stage Aaltonen had driven away with the special clock! The doorhandle of his Mini had caught in the loop of the clock. The remaining competitors were timed by ordinary stop-watches but there were a number of discrepancies and the organisers decided in fairness to all competitors to cancel the stage. It was tough luck on Jim Clark who dropped from sixth to ninth but the positions of the first three were unaffected.

Jim Clark's gallant bid virtually came to an end when he hit a pile of rocks on the Loch Achray stage and lost maximum marks, dropping him out of the first twenty. His Ford suffered severe damage to the front suspension but after hurried repairs, Clark was able to continue although his chance of honours had evaporated.

The outstanding Makinen was still setting a pace no one could match and held a comfortable five minutes lead over Soderstrom. Lindberg was still third and Britain's Paddy Hopkirk and Tony Fall fourth and fifth.

Then came final disaster for Jim Clark. On the Glengap stage, outside Dumfries, his Ford overturned. The crew were OK but that was the end of Jim's rally.

There was better fortune for Rauno Aaltonen. He drove into the Dumfries control to learn that back home in Finland his wife had given birth to a son.

It was to be the only good news for the BMC team for a while. At that point, they were the only manufacturers team left in the event but at Kielder Forest, near Otterburn, Hopkirk retired with a sheared drive-shaft and for the first time in the history of 'The Rally of the Forests' every manufacturers team had been eliminated.

The next night brought dramatic developments. Makinen, after leading the field for 1,600 miles was out, his Mini Cooper blowing up; Toivonen, reigning Finnish rally champion, was out having lost oil pressure; Hopkirk was out; so was the Italian ace Leo Cella; and the biggest surprise of all, three-time winner Erik Carlsson also had to retire.

And as the cars approached the breakfast halt at Barnby Moore, *137*

Lindberg, who had been in the first three for the major part of the Rally, retired with gearbox trouble.

So the order became Soderstrom (Ford), Orrenius (Saab) and Fall (Mini Cooper). Sylvia Osterberg was leading for the ladies' award but was being hotly chased by Pat Moss.

When Soderstrom came into Barnby Moor 14 minutes ahead of the field he found a birthday cake awaiting him. It was his 35th birthday and with only the Sherwood Forest and Silverstone tests before the finish, he looked like having something to really celebrate about.

Celebrate he did. The Ford was still ahead at London Airport and Soderstrom gave much of the credit for victory to his co-driver, Gunnar Palm, who had held him in check throughout 'driving at seven tenths instead of ten tenths' was how he put it. Indeed, few could dispute that Palm had good claim to being the best co-driver in the business — he had in the past

1966 winners: Bengt Soderstrom and Gunnar Palm (Ford). Soderstrom celebrated his 35th birthday during the event

teamed with two previous winners, Carlsson and Trana. Victory also gave Ford the World Rally Championship but although British cars had not only won but also finished second, fourth and fifth, the driving honours again went to Scandinavia with ten of the first twelve pilots coming from across the North Sea.

There was one hard luck story still to come. With the Ladies Award comfortably in her grasp, Sylvia Osterberg's Renault blew a cylinder head gasket at Silverstone and water poured from the engine. Sylvia kept going to the finish but had to stop every five miles to pour water into the boiling engine. It was too big a handicap and she was pipped on the post by Pat Moss, the seventh time Pat had won the prize.

1967 should have seen the RAC Rally in its finest hour. Again sponsored by the *Sun*, the event attracted a good entry which included Graham Hill, undeterred by his previous experience. Toivonen, Munari, Elford, Carlsson, Ove Andersson, Soderstrom (the 1966 winner), Cella, Aaltonen, Piot, Makinen, Hopkirk, Fall, Trana, Kallstrom, that redoubtable trio of women drivers, Pat Moss, Sylvia Osterberg and Rosemary Smith and almost any 'name' rally driver you care to mention.

The *Sun* had its own entry – a Renault, driven by Jennifer Nadin and motoring reporter Anne Hope.

Above all, and largely through the enthusiasm of ATV's Bill Ward, himself a regular competitor in international events, commercial television had mounted the biggest coverage ever planned of a British motoring event. With the co-operation of the various regional companies, TV planned regular daily programmes which would bring the rally into almost every home in Britain. Months of planning had gone into the venture, special equipment and control centres had been set up and a number of the entries were carrying an additional passenger – a camera-man – beginning with car No. 1, an Austin 1800, driven by the Towcester dairyman, Bob Freeborough. Bill himself could not compete this time – he was too busy masterminding the operation.

Then foot and mouth disease broke out in Britain's farming communities. At first it was thought that this would necessitate only a few changes in the route – after all, it had happened before. But day after day the situation got worse. Jack Kemsley and his organisers worked around the clock. Section after section had to be deleted. The overnight halt at Blackpool had to be cancelled. Still the disease spread.

Road books were altered, new signs erected. The Ministry of Agriculture, the Forestry Commission and the police leaned over backwards to help. **139**

The blow fell the night before the start. The Ministry telephoned to say that they were sending one of their top men to talk with us at Rally headquarters. The hotel was crowded with Press and television commentators, everyone wanting to know if the Rally was to be run or not? RAC officials and *Sun* executives adjourned to a private suite with the man from the Ministry and 'Willie' Williams, a *Sun* promotion man, stood guard on the door.

The Ministry man was brief and to the point. There was no sign of a halt to the spread of foot-and-mouth disease. If the Rally took place, it could be that it would help to spread the disease more quickly and over a wider area. The Ministry could not forbid us to run the event and they would not dream of trying to tell us that we could not. The facts had been placed on the table. The decision was up to us.

I looked around the room. There was Lord Camden, John Gott, Jack Kemsley, Dean Delamont. I don't think any of us really thought there was a choice. J. Duncan Campbell, an Odhams director and the man who had originally taken the decision re sponsorship, spoke: 'As far as the *Sun* is concerned, cancellation seems the only possible decision.' Agreement came from all quarters although for both the RAC and the *Sun,* it meant heavy financial loss.

I walked outside to give the bad news to the waiting journalists: Barrie Gill rushed to a telephone to stop the presses producing a Rally supplement which would now be so much waste paper. It must have broken the advertising boys' hearts. It certainly hit hard all of us in that room, not least Jack, who right up to the last moment had sweated blood to try and stage the event.

There was a little sequel some weeks later. Dean Delamont, Duncan Campbell and I met in Duncan's office. The *Sun,* said Duncan, felt that they should honour their obligation and reimburse the RAC for any losses incurred. Dean and I looked at one another – and politely declined. I like to think that all parties involved in the 1967 'disaster' did the right and the honourable thing.

If anything, the cancellation spurred everyone on to greater efforts in 1968. The entry list was, however, badly hit by the proximity of a special event, the London to Sydney Marathon, sponsored by the *Daily Express.* For the first time in many a long year, Ford, BMC, and Rootes gave the RAC Rally a miss, concentrating all their efforts on the Marathon. But there was still plentiful support for the RAC from overseas manufacturers including Lancia, Saab, Porsche and the East German Wartburgs. Fords produced a

A roadside rebuild: the unusual rally stickers indicate that it was during the period the old Sun newspaper sponsored the RAC

special incentive scheme for entrants of their cars and, all in all, it looked as if for once the 'privateers' would come into their own.

A complication was provided by the current international regulations which precluded the non-standard but very spectacular prototype cars.

In consequence, the RAC had to run another event concurrently for prototypes, a rally within a rally as it were, called the European Club Rally. Not unnaturally, it somewhat confused the issue and Lancias, for example, felt very hard done by when their Rauno Aaltonen, leading the Club rally, got virtually no publicity, although the times he was putting up were faster than those of the leaders in the RAC Rally itself. But, of course, press attention was concentrated on the main event.

Ninety-one special stages were planned making the 1968 RAC, on paper at least, the toughest yet. Most of them were again on forest land but the race circuits at Thruxton, Ingliston, Mallory Park and Silverstone were included. Start and finish were in London but this time the overnight halt was to be in Edinburgh although Blackpool was on the itinerary.

There were the usual alarums and excursions before the start. Gale force winds littered four of the Scottish stages in the Holy Loch area of Argyll with fallen trees and these had to be cut out of the route. It still left competitors to face more than 400 miles of forest roads in their 2,500 mile journey.

The Minister of Transport, Mr Richard Marsh, braved icy winds to flag the cars away from the Centre Airport Hotel at Longford (Middx.) and soon reports came back of tremendous crowds of spectators on the first special stages. It proved a recipe for disaster. At Hawley Common, near Camberley, normally used as a testing ground for tanks, 24-year-old company director, Tony Chappell, driving a Ford Escort, crashed and four people, including two children, were injured.

Chappell's co-driver, Hywel Thomas, was one of those taken to hospital.

Afterwards, Chappell, Welsh Rally winner and Television Rally-cross Champion said: 'There were between two and three thousand spectators lining this stage and at this point they were standing three to four deep. They were so close to the track it was ridiculous. A marshal told me that they had spent three hours trying to keep the crowds back and clear of the track'.

There were glum faces at Rally HQ where one could not help thinking that the Rally had developed a jinx. Fortunately, the injured all recovered and no similar accident marred the subsequent proceedings.

The Swedish ace, Bjorn Waldegard (Porsche) took an early lead and behind came the familiar figure of Timo Makinen, unusually not in a works car but in a privately-entered Ford Escort. It did not seem to make much difference to the fury of his driving.

Cars were soon dropping out. Alan Allard's Escort went off the track on a special stage and Lars Ytterbring (Cooper) retired with a cracked sump.

By the time they reached Bristol that evening, the official placings showed quite a few shocks. Waldegard limped into Bristol with just three minutes to spare and looked out of the running as mechanics worked furiously on his car. Locked for the lead were two more Swedes, Kallstrom (Lancia) and Lindberg (Saab) with the pursuing Makinen hard on their heels. Two more Saabs, with Trana and Orrenius at the wheels, came next. At this stage, the parallel European Club Rally looked something of a Lancia benefit, with Aaltonen first and Munari second.

The fast pace was taking its toll as the cars headed into North Wales. With drivers going flat out to beat their target times over the special stages, 27 of the original starters had already retired and only 85 were still running.

Trana had gone and so had Tony Fall. But progressing up the standings was Monte Carlo Rally winner, Vic Elford, in a works Porsche. Pat Moss

142

went off on a stage but although her Lancia was damaged she carried on.

As they neared the end of the Welsh section the order was Kallstrom, Makinen, Lampinen and Elford. But there was still a long, long way to go.

Kallstrom took nearly twenty minutes on one special stage and lost the lead in no uncertain manner. As they neared a rest-halt at Blackpool, it was Makinen the leader, followed by Lampinen, Orrenius and Elford. Fifth was an 'unknown' British driver, Chris Sclater, from Lewes (Sussex) driving in only his second international rally but handling his Lotus Cortina like a veteran. Lancias were first, second and third in the Club event with Aaltonen's total time just two seconds faster than Makinen's.

Sixty-four cars left Blackpool, only just over half the original field. Amongst them was the only all-woman crew surviving, Bronwy Burrell, of Hindhead (Surrey) and her co-driver, Joan Pink. Pat Moss had finally to retire after the earlier damage her car had suffered.

And not for the first time in the history of the event, the East German Wartburgs were leading for the Manufacturers Award.

A confident Timo was the first to arrive at Turnberry. He said he had had a good run and had not lost much time anywhere, his only misfortune being a ripped exhaust system which mechanics quickly repaired.

Meanwhile, Edinburgh police said the toughest section competitors would now have to face would be the last mile before the overnight halt in Scotland's capital. The first cars were due to arrive in the City about 5.30 pm, the peak of the rush hour, and a police spokesman said, 'We shall do our very best to help the Rally cars but I am afraid that some of them are bound to experience delays.'

Again Makinen was an early arrival but his battered car had 'enjoyed' all sorts of running repairs including the ingenious and liberal use of luggage straps. His lead was still intact but had narrowed to only 27 seconds over second-place Simo Lampinen. Orrenius was still third and Elford fourth.

Back in London, the organisers were re-crating many of the event's 100-odd major trophies. What is generally recognised as one of the world's toughest motoring events had already eliminated 60 of the 112 cars which had started and the Rally was only half-completed. One of the East German Wartburgs had dropped out, thus eliminating the only team left in the Manufacturers contest and the retirement of two Civil Service entries meant that there could be no Club team award either.

Drizzle and the morning rush hour greeted the 52 survivors as they left Edinburgh. One, Alan Main, a Macclesfield (Cheshire) farmer, did not go far. His Saab was pushed across the start-line and immediately jacked-up for *143* repairs to take place.

Vic Elford's Grand Prix racing experience stood him in good stead on the greasy Ingliston race circuit and although he did not look nearly so spectacular as Makinen in action, his time proved to be 18 seconds faster than that of the Rally leader.

Two more cars dropped out, one of them a Cooper, driven by John Capps, of Bawtry (Yorks) which hit a wall near Carnwath. No one was hurt.

Then, perhaps not unexpectedly, Timo's magnificent performance ended as it had so often ended on the RAC Rally, with the car not equal to the demands of the driver. After leading for nearly 1,000 miles, the 'Flying Finn' dropped out with a broken cylinder-head gasket and his fellow-countryman, Simo Lampinen (Saab) took over as front-runner.

Thick fog now added to the difficulties and amongst the competitors who failed to arive on time at the Chollerford (Northumberland) Control were

A Ford Cortina on the 1965 Rally with a rather re-arranged front end

Elford and Kallstrom. Bronwy Burrell did not turn up and nor did the Italian champion, Sandro Munari. Aaltonen, leading the European Club Rally, had crashed but was unhurt, thus eliminating all of the five Lancias.

With the Yorkshire Moors ahead, only 38 cars were reported still running, the leader-board being Lampinen, Orrenius, Jim Bullough, Phil Cooper, Bob Freeborough and Bruce Wilkinson and, in truth, it looked as if for once the private entries were going to get some of the glory. With the Lancias gone, another privateer, Rod Cooper, was leading the European event.

The fog had proved the deciding factor and as the 37 cars left tackled the six stages remaining before the London finish, it was pretty obvious that Lampinen with a 16 minute lead over Orrenius, had only to keep going to win. Three-quarters of an hour behind, came 41-year-old estate agent, Jim Bullough, the 1967 National Rally Champion.

Also in contact with the trees on the same event is the Rover 2000 of Logan Morrison and Johnstone Syer....note that string has its uses....

The Saabs of Lampinen and Orrenius reached Mallory Park at midday and so confident were the Saab team now that, although two stages remained, the cars were washed and polished in readiness for their triumphant return.

The confidence was not misplaced. The final results showed the works Saabs first and second, an East German Wartburg seventh − and every one of the other leading positions filled by private entries. And private entries had finished 1-2-3 in the European Club event. Sixteen cars had started in this event − only three finished. Ninety-six had started in the Rally proper, only 32 had finished.

The forests − and the fog − had done their work...

The Back Room Boys

FIVE HUNDRED dinners and five hundred breakfasts — most of them to be served in the bedrooms — is the sort of not-so-casual order that the manager of the Station Hotel, Perth, was passing down to the kitchens on the afternoon of Tuesday, November 10th, 1964.

It's the sort of thing which makes a chef wish he'd taken up something peaceful — like drilling holes in the road or being manager for the Beatles — but it's a situation which has to be faced when your hotel is selected by the organisers of the RAC British International Rally as an overnight stop.

In fact, hotel staff are often the unsung heroes of an international rally. Rally business comes with a rush, around 150 drivers, 150 navigators, the trade boys, officials and even wives, sweethearts and husbands — of the competitors, most of them wanting immediate service after cramped and weary hours in a car.

It usually requires every bit of resource and courtesy, every last man and woman on the hotel staff, for any hotel to cope. And it is a great tribute to most of the hotels which have been used as rally headquarters or halts by the RAC, that complaints from the recipients of their service have been few and far between. Occasionally, a hotel has failed to grasp the size of the task and there has been dissatisfaction all round but these occasions have indeed been few.

In recent years, the start and finish hotel has also been Rally headquarters throughout the week and, although these days there are always a number of **147** specially installed direct lines to Rally HQ itself, to the Results Team and to the Press Office, the hotel switchboard girls still bear a heavy load with thousands of telephone calls, in and out.

Stage results pour in by telephone and teleprinter. Problems have to be solved over the wires. The world's press will be ringing continuously – and any RAC Press Officer will tell you that in Sweden, Finland and France, newspapermen simply never go to bed. And when somebody is wanted and can't be found then the hotel staff usually have to swing into action via the switchboard or public address system. Personally, I've always liked the 'bleeper' system first used at the Imperial Hotel, Blackpool, a frequent RAC Rally venue. All key officials are given a small gadget which slips into the breast pocket like a handkerchief. Then, if you're wanted, a 'bleep-bleep' signal is transmitted and you can hurry to the nearest telephone. Mark you, the thing can 'bleep-bleep' in the most darned awkward places...

...And old ladies in restaurants are likely to ask to be moved to a table further away from that strange young man...

Hotels along the route which are used as breakfast halts also have their problems. Often these are smaller establishments and the task of providing hundreds of bacon-and-eggs is a formidable one. And often hundreds of spectators, in addition to the competitors, are liable to invade the hotel in search of food, drink, telephone calls – and anything else which hotels normally provide. The rush at these places where time is so fleeting often makes Oxford Circus look like a peaceful backwater.

Naturally enough, the hotel people are not the only unsung heroes of the Rally. For more than a week, some 2,000 folk will be busy on duties connected with the event. Four hundred control marshals, for instance. Another 250 checking results, keeping the score, organising the prize-giving and Rally ball, keeping the Press informed, adjudicating on disputes. Hundreds of policemen and local authority officials, works service teams, filling station attendants, RAC patrols, radio reporters, television and newsreel cameramen.

Between them all, they will cover millions of miles, make hundreds of telephone calls, distribute something like one hundred thousand circulars, Press hand-outs and programmes.

From a rag-bag of memories, some stories of the backroom boys...

Not surprisingly, some of my own Rally memories concern the activities of fellow PROs. One year, Alan Powell, then with Rootes, gained his firm a great deal of publicity working hard and 'feeding' the Press with some good stories. Radar traps were in the news and Alan came up with the answer: the

Lombard as main sponsors have added a high degree of gloss to the Rally in recent years. A prize-giving at York — the author (on left in white jacket) and Jack Kemsley on extreme right. Sir Clive Bossom hands over an award and Neal Eason-Gibson gets the next trophy ready

Rootes teams' star driver, Tiny Lewis, had a device fitted to the front of this car which picked up radar signals and defeated radar traps. The story made headlines, police and Post Office officials had a fit, and while Tiny, in all innocence, sped on his way in the Rally, talk of 'arrests' and 'prosecutions' flooded the Blackpool control.

Alan got his story but one PRO who didn't — and to spare him further blushes, he will remain anonymous — was the PRO for a well-known safety-belt firm. At the end of the 1961 RAC, Press and Trade were allowed to 'have a go' at the speed tests on Madeira Drive. The PRO had a 'go' to such effect that he 'pranged' somebody else's MG Midget. Nor could he find anyone to believe his explanation: 'My foot jammed under the brake.'   **149**

Long-time BBC radio commentator, Robin Richards, more recently with LBC, is a chap who has done quite a lot for rallying in this country with his regular broadcasts during the RAC over many years. Robin, once known for some reason which escapes me now, as 'Dr Morrell', is always good fun and has whiled away many of the small, dark hours from his repertoire of funny stories.

But there was one time when the rest of us didn't think he was so funny. It was in the days when Rally headquarters moved around the country instead of staying put in one place. Jack Kemsley worked it out that with this particular itinerary it would be impossible for headquarters staff to drive from place to place as usual. Instead, the services of British Railways would have to be invoked.

So, late in the evening, after the Rally cars had left Blackpool, hire cars transported six or seven of us, including Jack, Robin Richards and yours truly to Preston Station where we were supposed to pick up a connection for Inverness.

Will Hay, on the ticket barrier, was quite definite. 'The 11.45? That went at 10.45. The next one, in about an hour and a quarter.'

'What are we going to do on Preston Station for more than an hour,' someone asked.

A good question. The buffet was closed. The waiting room fire was almost out. And any moment, unless British Railways put another shilling in the meter, it looked as if all the lights would go out too.

Then spake up Dr Morell. 'I know,' he beamed, 'let's go to a night club.'

For all I know, Preston may these days boast some night clubs. But this was nearly 20 years ago.

Robin and I have shared many rally vigils since then but the only times we ever fell out were at the start of the Rally when the BBC microphones sometimes picked up the booming 'croak' of Drackett pontificating over the public address system. 'It's bad enough competing with the bloody aeroplanes,' says Robin, 'without having your voice drowning my commentary.'

Says I snidely, 'Use my commentary and save paying Richards a fee.'

Says Robin's producer, Arthur Phillips: 'But we like to get the facts right.'

A red-faced moment behind the mike was several years earlier. The finish was at Hastings and I was to interview the first arrival for BBC Television News. It turned out to be a past winner, Lyndon Sims. Lyndon, one of the nicest chaps in rallying, loves a good old natter. And my wife laughs cynically if someone describes me as a quiet man. So, with the microphone between us, Lyndon and I chattered away happily.

Vaguely, from the corner of my eye, I noticed someone apparently waving at me. It was Vic, the cameraman. 'Very nice interview,' he said, 'but we ran out of film five minutes ago.'

Unipart, a BL subsidiary, were supporting sponsors during the Mirror newspaper era. Here, Dick Nelson of Unipart, hands over a cheque to Phil Drackett outside the Royal Station Hotel at York. John Lewsey, of the Mirror, looks on

Sometimes violence rears its ugly head. In the heat and stress and strain tempers are lost and 'punch ups' are not unknown. I've seen 'pushing matches' between competitor and competitor, between team manager and driver and, one year, a certain well-known PRO had his hands around the throat of a certain well-known journalist. And I don't think he intended to kiss him.

One little incident concerned a Swedish driver and my wife. Now, 'Beanball' (and don't ask me to explain how she got that nickname because it's a long story) has a much more pleasant personality than her husband and we often utilised her services in soothing irate customers. She's so good at it that she's universally popular with the Press boys who regularly cover the rally and the Swedish journalists in particular. In fact one of them, Lars Olof Magnil, always brings her a wooden horse at each Rally. If he keeps it up we shall soon have to move to a larger house.

But the Swedish journalists speak English. And this driver didn't. I came into the Press Office to find Beanball seated on one side of the table, the Swede on the other. The Swede was shouting and pounding the table with his fist. Beanie was nearly in tears. 'I'm trying to explain to him that if he wants to complain about the Rally rules, he must go to the Rally Control not the Press Office,' she said, 'and he's being horrid about it.'

'How dare you speak to my wife like that,' says me.

The Swede stood up. Now I'm a big man but this fellow was like Carnera. He unfolded by the yard. When the top of his blond crew-topped head reached around eight feet, I sat down.

'Let's be reasonable about this,' I said.

The finish at Bournemouth one year coincided with the birthday of 'Scoop' Russell, chief of the Rally Results team. After the prize-giving, Scoop threw another party back at the hotel. The champagne flowed, the faint hearts retreated to their rooms and 'Beanball' and her friend, Margaret Beaney (no relation), otherwise known as 'Scoop's' secretary and (on the Rally) typist-in-chief to the Results team, decided to give a dancing display. It was around four in the morning.

A porter came in with another armful of champagne. 'Twenty-two pounds, please sir,' he said.

'I didn't order any more champagne.'

'Sir, two girls in blue just danced through the front hall and said, "Send in more champagne".'

'Then let the two girls in blue pay for it.'

A remarkable girl this Mrs Beaney.

The Centre Airport Hotel left two large clothes racks in the Press Room during the 1968 Rally. To the eagle eye of Mrs Beaney they made a very acceptable trapeze and one night she was discovered performing all manner of somersaults and 'loop the loop' exercises.

The inhabitants of the Press Office thought about charging entertainment tax. Her boss, 'Scoop' Russell was so proud of her that he started bringing spectators in to see his remarkable secretary.

Not that the Results team normally gets much time for relaxation. They usually put in a fantastic amount of work, day and night, surviving on coffee and sandwiches. One year a computer firm offered to run a results service for the rally. It was decided to give it a whirl but the precaution was taken of maintaining the usual service as well. Fortunately, as it happened, since the human team invariably beat the mechanical marvel by about an hour. (In recent years a computer system has been successful). Sometimes there is ill-founded criticism about results being slow. On the rare occasions when this does occur it is invariably because of human error and one of the many voluntary marshals charged with the job of telephoning through stage results has failed to do so at the appointed time.

No international rally would get far without the service crews — just take a look at what this bunch is doing....

It is not unknown for a marshal to toddle off to breakfast with the results in his pocket, having forgotten that at Rally HQ officials are awaiting them anxiously. But normally speaking, a leader-board is ready for the Press within thirty minutes of the completion of each stage, which is quite something when one bears in mind that some of these stages are many miles from telephones and that the cavalcade of rally cars takes approximately three hours to negotiate each stage.

'Scoop's' right-hand man on many a Rally was 'Putt' otherwise Ron Putland. One year Ron and I motored together on the Rally, he as Results Official, me a travelling Press Officer. It was a hard slog through fog, rain and snow with constant telephoning, picking up result cards in one place and putting them on trains at main line stations and so on.

Ron's timetable for the final day of the Rally will give you some idea of just how hard the backroom boys work.

5.30 am	Out of bed to take up duty at the Control in the Queen's Hotel, Cheltenham. No breakfast − no time. Working until...
12.30 midday	Then drive to Prescott, eight miles away, to pick up result sheets of hill-climb tests there. No lunch − no time. Drive back to London, arriving...
3.40 pm	At Rally HQ, this year located in the Club House of the RAC at Pall Mall. Work on collating and tabulating provisional placings on road section. Waitress brings coffee and sandwiches.
Midnight	With all provisional results stencilled and duplicated, drive girl assistants home, then into bed, ready to start work again at 8.30 next morning.

So whilst our homburg is tilted respectfully to the competitors, the hundreds of willing helpers who make the whole thing possible should also be spared a passing thought.

One invaluable backroom boy over the years has been Peter Cooper, himself a competitor of no mean repute. Apart from his abilities as a rally driver, Peter is a whizz hand at hurling cars around restricted places with the judicious use of the handbrake − in other words, driving tests − and was once the regular wicket-keeper for a Hampshire cricket team until succeeded by a gentleman lately retired from county cricket, one Godfrey Evans.

Peter is built like a rugger forward rather than a wicket-keeper and at

A spectator control unit, one of the Ford vehicles designed to help with the massive problem of crowd control on today's rallies

times this has been more than useful at post-rally celebrations. There was one year at Bournemouth when matters started to get out of hand and rolls and water-pistols began to do their dastardly work. However, the appearance of Peter and a few other characters of similarly deterrrent physique, speedily quietened the trouble-makers. But even Peter & Co. couldn't prevent a grand piano being hoisted into a swimming pool the year the Rally finished at Brighton. That little exploit cost the organisers around £300.

And talking of pianos, there was another occasion when the last of the revellers went to bed leaving one determined little gentleman still seated on the piano singing. When everyone came down to breakfast he was still on the piano but by now he was fast asleep. No one bothered to wake him and for all I know he may still be there.

The 'hard core' of the backroom organisation for many years, if such a term can be applied to such charming people, is the rest of the Kemsley family − Jack's wife Joan, daughters Ann and Sally and son John. Not only were they roped in to help during the Rally itself but they had to live with it for the rest of the year, the Kemsley house being liberally bespattered with maps, regulations, entry forms and what have you.

155

But they are remarkably good-tempered and a very united family, the measure of their achievements being that father Jack was, at Christmas 1969, nominated by the *Sunday Times* as 'the motor sport organiser of the decade'.

However, their affection for the 'old man' was given a severe testing on the 1966 Rally when the police telephoned HQ and said they had arrested a man who claimed to be Jack Kemsley, organiser of the RAC Rally. His offence? – stealing a car.

It was all sorted out in the end but what had happened was this: Jack had left HQ, stepped into his car and moved off. Three angry men immediately ran after him, shouting and waving. Jack saw them in his mirror and stopped. They ran up and two of them pulled Jack from the car telling the third to fetch a policeman.

It transpired that there were two identical Ford Zephyrs in the hotel car park and the keys of each fitted the other. Jack had chosen the wrong one.

It took him a long time to live down that little episode.

A red face to match for Ken Dennis, who for several years held the Night Watch in the Rally Press Office. One night he sat into the small hours with an attractive lady reporter helping her to write a feature on the Rally. Next day when he came into the office there was a notice on the board, signed by the young lady in question and surrounded by a host of grinning readers. It said simply: 'Message for Ken Dennis: Thank you for what you did for me last night – it was wonderful.' Ken has felt misunderstood ever since.

Another pillar of the Rally in the sixties was policeman, John Gott.

John 'lost' the car on a mountain pass. 'To my unutterable relief as the car went over the edge I saw that the drop was only about twenty-five feet into a meadow and not 2,000 feet into space. Bill Shepherd, my No. 2, was magnificent. All he said as we went over was, "You know, John, you've done that all wrong." The perfect team-mate.'

John drove the car down through an unfenced meadow for some 300 yards, bounced into a ploughed field, drove another 200 yards along this and so back on to the road. And after all that they finished the rally third in their class.

That's what rallying is all about.

Anatomy of a Rally

THERE ARE two programmes in existence for the 1969 RAC International Rally of Great Britain. One, now a rarity since the bulk quantity was disposed of as waste paper, is printed in blue and orange and bears the legend 'sponsored by the *Sun*'. It also includes a full-page about the *Sun* newspaper and various other references. The other, not such a rarity since thousands of copies were sold to the many spectators of the Rally, is printed in blue-and-white and try as you may you will not find a reference to the *Sun* anywhere therein.

And thereby hangs a tale which illustrates the behind-the-scenes difficulties of sports promotions which the public and, very often, even the competitors don't realise exist.

The anatomy of the 1969 Rally differed in many respects from other years and yet in other ways it was typical of the cliff-hanging crises which abound wherever in the world international rallies are run.

The *Sun* newspaper had come to the rescue of the RAC Rally a few years previously when the Rally itself was threatened with extinction by ever-rising costs. A chance conversation between Barrie Gill, the paper's then motoring correspondent, and the present writer led to a partnership which was in every way a most harmonious one and enabled the Rally to become even more successful as an international event.

But as 1969 dawned, it was not the future of the Rally which was threatened but that of the *Sun* itself. The paper had arisen from the ashes of the old *Daily Herald* but everyone knew that despite its bright image the harsh realities of newspaper economics were making the struggle for survival a difficult one. Only the fact that it was part of the giant International

Publishing Corporation empire was keeping the *Sun* burning and in Fleet Street the question was: how long will IPC continue to bolster the paper?

It was against this background that RAC officials met with executives of Odhams Newspapers, the IPC subsidiary which controlled the *Sun* (and the very successful *People,* not to mention the *Sporting Life*) to discuss the continued sponsorship of the Rally. We of the RAC were not worried about the possibility of being without a sponsor − the great success the Rally had enjoyed in recent years meant that there were several other suitors for our hand awaiting in the wings. We were worried about still increasing costs amounting to thousands of pounds and arising in the main from the use of Forestry Commission land. Not to use this land would rob the Rally of its character but, at the same time, the RAC was determined that in fairness to all other forms of motor sport coming under its control, the Rally must at least be self-supporting. Moreover, the partnership with the *Sun* had, as I said earlier, been a happy one and we felt that we had a moral obligation if not a legal one to continue with the *Sun* as sponsor if at all possible.

A lunch or two at the Connaught Rooms and at the RAC in Pall Mall, a few dozen telephone calls and a score of letters later, agreement had been reached. The *Sun* would sponsor the 1969 Rally.

A month or two later, everything seemed to be in the melting-pot again when it became known that IPC had regretfully decided that the *Sun* would cease publication at the end of the year. True, the Rally was in November but what newspaper would wish to embark upon a major promotion within a few weeks of its own demise? And what would be the point of it as far as the newspaper itself was concerned?

To the RAC the possibility of being without a sponsor was now a reality, a serious reality since we realised that our other potential sponsors would not be anxious at this late stage to step in with a rescue operation which would not enable them to extract full value from their sponsorship.

We need not have worried. Hard on the heels of the announcement of the *Sun's* impending demise, the telephone rang in my office and over the wire crackled the re-assurance from an Odham's executive that IPC would honour their commitment to the RAC.

Large organisations and the tycoons who run them often come under fire and are accused of all sorts of shenanigans from time to time. There's another side to most of them and the conduct of the International Publishing Corporation in honouring what was more of a gentleman's agreement than a hard-and-fast contract shows that in British business at least there is still **158** room for the old-fashioned institution of straight dealing.

So everything went ahead. Regulations, programmes, press release paper, rally plates and armbands, were all printed.

Then the cat was amongst the pigeons in a big way. Rupert Murdoch, Australian 'whizz-kid' owner of the *News of the World,* made a bid for the *Sun* and just a few weeks before the Rally was scheduled to begin, the newspaper changed hands. Moreover, it was to be re-launched as a tabloid under the Murdoch banner bang in the middle of the Rally.

There was no problem re the sponsorship which would continue from IPC. There was a problem about the vast amount of material which had been printed carrying the *Sun* emblem and name.

Regulations were easy. All likely competitors had had them weeks ago and there was nothing to be done about it. Press releases were no problem. We just dropped the special Rally paper and carried on using the normal RAC press release headings. Armbands, fortunately, did not carry the *Sun* emblem anyway. The Rally plates (to go on the front of all competing, official and press cars) did but the emblem was a one end of the plate to balance the RAC badge at the other. The plates themselves were of a plastic fabric type and a day's work with a dozen pairs of scissors and some willing hands soon removed all evidence of the *Sun.*

The programmes were a different matter − and only the valiant efforts of a sweating Home Counties printer and his men produced the revised publication in time for the start.

That's why there are two different programmes for the 1969 Rally.

Oddly enough, the new *Sun* almost completely ignored the Rally, which could have been a mistake, since there must have been many thousands of people throughout the country still under the impression that the Rally was *Sun*-sponsored and disappointed when they found no news of the event in that paper.

Although for obvious reasons the promotional activities of the IPC group were to be muted, the *Daily Mirror* launched a competition, the winner of which would receive the Ford car driven in the Rally by Roger Clark. This naturally added to the interest and everything worked out well when the competition was won by an Army sergeant keenly interested in the sport who had worked in service crews on many an event. And he was most diffident in his daily enquiries as to whether Roger − not to mention the car − was still in one piece. Both survived to the finish, as it happened, and the Army man duly got his reward.

Lombank too gave their regular support to the event in the shape of the expensive-to-produce road books and other aids necessary to the *159* organisation while Shell came up with a plan to help the private entries.

All entrants driving their own cars and using Shell products were eligible for an additional £900 in prize money 'to encourage the private rally motorist who is literally running on his own against the sponsored works teams.'

You might think that all that was enough excitement for one year but not a bit of it. What followed was all in the day's work.

To start with, it rained torrentially the day before the cars were due to leave the Centre Airport Hotel, near London Airport. (So near indeed, that the 'planes seemed just a few feet over your head and at one stage when I was doing the public-address commentary as the cars returned to the finish the following Wednesday, I was moved to remark... 'as I was saying when I was so rudely interrupted by TWA'). You may wonder why the fuss about some rain before the start? Ask the scrutineers in their big, damp and draughty marquee as they try to check all the details of the competing cars. Ask the competitors themselves as they queue up for scrutineering. Ask the RAC patrols and marshals as they erect barriers, put up signs and generally get everything in order for the morrow.

Saturday itself hardly dawned bright and fair but at least was an improvement on the previous day. Yet the dark clouds and lowering skies must have frightened some people away. The crowd was a good one but not as big as the previous year.

So as 11 am came around, the first of the cars left. This was one of the new Triumphs, driven by Andrew Cowan, winner of the London to Sydney Marathon. There was a great deal of interest in these big 6-cylinder cars and even more conjecture on how they would fare in the forests. Team manager Peter Browning said, 'We are entering the Triumphs in the RAC Rally as a warmer for the London to Mexico World Cup Rally in which we will be using three Triumph 2.5 Mk2's. The RAC Rally will provide us with an excellent opportunity to train both the crews and mechanics in readiness for the World Cup Rally.'

Earlier in the year, single Triumph 2.5 PI entries in both the Alpine and Scottish Rallies had indicated that the cars certainly had rally potential. 'The petrol injected Triumph will be one of the strongest cars in this year's Rally,' commented Peter, 'the harder the conditions the better it will suit us.'

In the sequel, the Triumphs certainly proved to be strong but not quite quick enough for some other cars which also proved to be strong. But that is to go ahead of the story. Meanwhile, it was a little moment of rally history since the last time a Triumph team had participated in an international rally *160* had been the Monte of 1966.

Two Triumphs — prototypes of the present 2.5 — had been prepared for the ill-fated 1967 RAC event and were to have been driven by the then world champion racing driver, Denny Hulme, and Roy Fidler.

So the crowd interest in Cowan and his car was great. Amongst other early starters to get attention was the Round Britain power-boat race winner, Timo Makinen, always good for an exciting performance in the RAC Rally, and his fellow Finn, the 1968 winner, Simo Lampinen.

Seated aloft in the giant Guards Cigarettes mobile unit which served as rest-lounge for weary marshals and commentary-box for me, it was interesting to study the different attitudes of the drivers. Some looked tense and worried, others relaxed and carefree.

Paddy Hopkirk and Tony Nash (Triumph 2.5 PI) in the ice and snow of the 1969 RAC

THE STORY OF THE RAC INTERNATIONAL RALLY

We try to give spectators as much information about the rally crews as possible and often the drivers respond with a cheery smile and a 'thumbs up' to the commentary box. Sometimes it isn't their thumbs that they use...

At least a couple of drivers on the 1969 Rally appreciated the commentator's remarks. Ron Harrison (Ford Escort) heard − not a dissertation on his car − but the virtues of his business extolled.

All spectators were recommended to visit the Clarendon restaurant at Weymouth next time they were in the area.

And Colin Barrell (Ford Cortina), a funeral director from Portsmouth, nodded his head in vigorous agreement when I surmised that 'he must be the fastest hearse-driver in the business'. But the gleeful grin on the face of Stanley Griffin (Car No. 84) when I wondered if the driver of Car No. 83 knew that a policeman was on his tail in No. 84, worries me. Did I put thoughts into the head of Stanley, a police officer stationed at Tooting? Did it suddenly occur to him that even if he did not win the Rally he might have a lot of fun knocking off his fellow competitors for speeding?

The real human story at the start concerned two competitors who got a special cheer to themselves. They were Mark Newman and Arthur Russell, both from South-East London, and driving a Lotus Cortina. Mark, a director of a company in the clothing trade, has a permanent leg disablement due to a rugger injury. Arthur, who works for Ford, has two artificial legs. It was the first time in the history of motor sport that a team of disabled drivers had competed in an international rally.

Mark had been rallying for nine years and for him it was his second international, his first having been the Gulf London Rally. For Arthur it was his international debut.

Mark said, 'The idea of doing the RAC in an invalid carriage − which is the legal classification for a car fitted out for a disabled driver − started as a bit of a giggle but suddenly it became serious.'

When he decided to have a go, his first problem was to find another disabled driver with an international licence. That's where Arthur came in.

The next problem was a car. Mark normally drives a Mini Cooper S but this was not big enough for the purpose. They approached Fords for a car. There was no spare available but a fellow-member of the Bexley Car Club came to the rescue with the loan of a twin-cam Lotus Cortina.

One firm provided a free set of rally tyres and another converted the controls without charge, the clutch being worked by a lever on top of the gear shift. It certainly foxed the scrutineers at the start since not surprisingly, international regulations do not say anything about invalid carriages.

Both men said that they hoped by entering the rally they would encourage other handicapped people. Without doubt they achieved that objective although, in the end, they failed to finish. They started extremely well but broke down on a special stage in Scotland and had to retire.

There were not too many headaches at the outset of the event. There was ice on 23 of the first 26 stages and a lot of competitors went out but that, after all, is what rallying is all about. Amongst those who fell by the wayside were some of the favourites including Timo Makinen, Hannu Mikkola, Simo Lampinen and Sandro Munari. Again that is what rallying is all about. (Try telling it, however, to a reporter on a certain national newspaper who telephoned to ask if we would abandon the Rally in view of the number of cars which were having to drop out? That is when hapless Press Officers beat their heads against the wall in despair.)

Only one mishap occurred on the admin. side at this point. Paddy Hopkirk, in his Triumph, suddenly shot to the top of the placings after a few stages. A suspicious official queried this and it was found that an error of marking of one minute in Paddy's favour on one of the stages accounted for his meteoric rise to the top. Discovery of the error precipitated an equally sudden descent for the popular Irishman.

In truth, no one expected Paddy and his team-mates, Cowan and Brian Culcheth, to win. Paddy himself, asked by a television reporter what was the most difficult thing about the Rally, replied, 'Winning in this car.' But as British Leyland had already said, the object of the exercise was a preliminary canter for the World Cup event. As it was, all three finished in the first 25, 1-2-3 in their class and 2nd in the Manufacturers Team Award. A good performance considering, as Team Manager Peter Browning said to me afterwards, 'All the time we were running Minis we prayed for these conditions. When we finally get them we're running big Triumphs.'

The Triumphs were to be edged out for the Manufacturers Award by the Japanese Datsuns, which were also making their international competition debut driven by a Finn, an Englishman and a Kenyan. Datsuns told me that their 'original' strategy was to win the team prize and, original or not, this was just what they did. They say that Rauno Aaltonen, the No. 1 driver, sent a cable home to Finland, 'We are not fast but we are strong.'

As the cars headed on into Scotland with Jack Kemsley and his helpers beaming happily in Rally Control; P.D. and his helpers beaming happily in the Press Office; and 'Scoop' Russell and his helpers beaming happily in the Results Office, something was building up which was rapidly going to wipe the beams off all their faces. That which was building up was — SNOW. *163*

Hotrod champion and speedway star, Barry Lee, with Peter Warren, in the Fordsport-entered Escort on the 1969 Rally

Tony Fall and Henry Liddon (Lancia), who eventually finished third, surrounded by snow in 1969

The Simonian-Phillips Datsun 1600 at St. Mary's Loch during the 1969 event

Kallstrom-Haggbom (Lancia) sideways on at Castle O'er en route to victory in 1969

Soon the reports were coming in from officials in charge of the North Wales area that snow was blocking many of the forest tracks. 'It's OK on the main roads,' said one, 'but above the snow-line it doesn't look as if there's a hope of the cars getting through.' Meanwhile, the surviving rally crews were headed for Blackpool and their one overnight rest during the event. Next morning they would be on their way to North Wales via the Oulton Park race circuit. Could the risk be taken of the entire rally bogging down in the snowy Welsh mountains? Another report came in. A marshal had tried to get through one of the special stages in a Land Rover and had failed.

The decision was taken. Peter Harper, the 1958 RAC winner, and his co-driver, David Pollard, who had been doing an official liaison job out on the route, were back at Headquarters, tired, weary and with red-rimmed eyes. But they were ready to help if they could by leaving for North Wales and attempting to get through. If Harper could get through, was the thought, then it would not be unreasonable to ask the competitors to make the effort (most people, I think, had the contretemps the year Burgess won, very much in their minds).

Came the question of a suitable car. Alan Zafer, Competitions Press Officer of British Leyland, volunteered a solution. There was a Triumph 2.5 similar to those taking part in the Rally, down the road at Abingdon, headquarters of the BLMC Competitions Department. It could be prepared in a few hours. The word was given and a phone call went through to the marshal-in-charge of North Wales to meet Harper and Pollard at some ungodly hour of the morning at some ungodly (if Welsh readers will pardon the expression) hole on a mountain road.

Here they were to pick up driving chains and a handful of officials armed with diversion boards. They would attempt to get through every doubtful stage but if they failed on one, an official would be left behind to divert the rally cars around the stage to the next one. Lucky official.

In the sequel, they got through but although conditions improved slightly in most places by the time the competitors got there, one stage at Clocaenog did become completely blocked and had to be by-passed.

Nor was that the end of the commotions. Rain and slush on main roads, traffic congestion caused by the cars of spectators and those of the general public who had no intention of being spectators, plus police diversions, caused havoc. The conditions, nothing to do with the Rally proper, were obviously bearing more heavily on some competitors than others and putting them at a disadvantage. So another decison was taken: this time to give an
166 hour's extra halt at Machynlleth which, apart from preventing any

What rallying is all about: wet, windy and dark – who wants Number Thirteen?

competitors being unfairly penalised, would enable everyone to freshen up and give an opportunity to check the cars before the still-tough stages which lay ahead.

Monte Carlo Rally winner, Bjorn Waldegard, driving a Porsche, was comfortably in the lead at this point and had indeed been in front since Saturday. He seemed certain of victory but in rallying, no less than horseracing, there is no such thing as a certainty. On the first special stage at Hafren, Waldegard lost it completely on a left-hand bend and ended up in the ditch, only the top of his car being visible to passers-by. Waldegard stayed with the car whilst his co-driver, Lars Helmer, ran back to find help. *167*

*In 1972, Roger Clark
and Tony Mason
(Escort) became the first
British drivers to win
the Rally since 1959*   **169**

He enlisted the aid of some spectators and the Porsche was retrieved from the ditch but the incident cost the Swede the maximum time for the stage plus a 20-minute penalty — and that comfortable five-minute lead over the field had more than disappeared. Now Harry Kallstrom, in one of the works Lancias, who had never been off the leader board since the start, took over in front and began to look as impregnable as Waldegard had appeared. Kallstrom was assured of the European Rally Championship whatever happened since his nearest rival, the Belgian Gilbert Staepelaere, had withdrawn at the last moment.

Waldegard had no intention of giving up without a fight but in his anxiety to make up lost ground, he 'overcooked it' again and this time lost another four minutes which put him right out of contention. Kallstrom (pronounced 'Shell-strom') was driving brilliantly and it became more and more obvious that, short of a Waldegard-type error, no one could catch him over the last — and comparatively easy — section. But behind him the battle for minor places was a fierce one with most attention focussed on the progress of Roger Clark (Ford). Way back in Scotland, Roger had commented that it was no use trying to tackle the Swedes on territory just made for them and that he was content to play a 'waiting game' until the latter stages. Now Clark was living up to his word and fighting his way up the standings. In the sequel, he had left his bid too late and had to be content with an honourable fifth place. The other struggle in the limelight was for the Manufacturers Team Award which lay between the British Triumphs and the Japanese Datsuns with Ford's 'reserve' team, the only other works survivor, tagging behind. The more-fancied Saab, Lancia and Ford No. 1 teams had all fallen by the wayside fairly early on. In fact, choosing your team can be one of the biggest difficulties facing a Team Manager. At one time in the 1969 RAC, Lancia had three cars in the first six yet if that had been the final finishing order they would not have won the team award. Reason? Lancias had four 'works' cars entered and a team is composed of three. Lancia nominated Kallstrom, Makinen and the Italian champion, Sandro Munari, as their trio. Makinen retired fairly early on. Munari also dropped out later. But Britisher Tony Fall, the man they left out of the official team, finished third. Football managers do not have a prerogative of headaches.

Thus it was Triumph v. Datsun on the home stretch and although at one time the Britishers snatched a narrow lead of a few seconds, the Datsuns came into the finish at the Centre Airport Hotel in line astern, 1-2-3, and happily nursing a comfortable advantage over their rivals.

170   The tumult and the shouting was not yet over. After the champagnebedoused Kallstrom and Gunnar Haggbom had accepted the winner's plaudits, controversy centred around the beaming figure of another Swedish driver, Hakan Lindberg, whose Saab had been up and down the standings like a yo-yo. At first it was decided to knock a minute off his time which put him into third place but, after a Steward's Enquiry, the minute was put back on again, restoring Tony Fall to third position. It was hardly less than Fall deserved. On the recent TAP Portugese Rally he had been disqualified on a technicality after appearing a comfortable winner. As he and co-driver Henry Liddon had neared the finishing line, the crowd swarmed forward. Liddon got out to check the position of the finish control and Fall's wife, who was in the crowd, was pressed against the car. To protect her from injury, Tony motioned her into the car — and was disqualified for carrying an unauthorised passenger. There was a stronger reason why he deserved third place on the RAC. One of the early stages had been scrubbed by the organisers after a competitor had stopped half-way through the stage then driven back down it in a Land Rover, a remarkably dangerous thing to do. Since about eighteen of the cars were still to go through the stage at that time, the organisers had no alternative but to eliminate it from the results. And easily the fastest man of those who did go through was Tony Fall. So much so that had his time counted he would have been undisputedly third whether or not Lindberg had been credited with the extra minute.

A Steward's Enquiry sounds ominous. In fact, it is a routine matter and the 1969 RAC Rally was the first for many years not to be followed by a protest — which is a much more serious affair.

So for once everyone was happy. Lancia had achieved an outright victory (and the empty champagne bottles were still in the Press Room next morning to prove it); Datsun had won the Team Award (and were now contemplating an all-out attack on the European rally scene); the British Leyland Triumphs had finished 1-2-3 in their class (a hollow victory if you like since only five cars started in that class but they had achieved what they set out to do — a successful preliminary canter for the 1970 World Cup Rally); and even the Czech Skoda boys were happy. Their works team had been prevented from coming by a fire at the factory but their lone privateer driven by Welsh garage proprietor, Mike Hinde, had finished and won its class.

And even Mrs Joan Pink was happy. Joan, widow of steeple-chase jockey, Trevor Pink was 69th and last. But that in itself is quite an achievement when 151 cars originally set off in such high hope. And, since only two all-women crews finished, Joan was runner-up for the Ladies Award.

THE STORY OF THE RAC INTERNATIONAL RALLY

As the after-rally party glowed dimly in the small hours of the morning, a bright and perky, pipe-smoking gent stepped into the Press Office. It was Philip Mulcahy, of the International Publishing Corporation.

'Now, Phil,' he said, 'what about next year's Rally?...

The Years Between

THE NEXT decade was to see many changes in the RAC Rally, not least the ascendancy of the British Ford Motor Company amongst the winners. And in the sponsorship field, the merchant bank Lombard, which had long supported the Rally to varying degrees, finally took over sole sponsorship in 1974.

The 1970 Rally, however, was sponsored by our rescuers the year before, the *Daily Mirror*, and was again based at the Centre Airport Hotel, London.

It was a gruelling event with the British weather doing its worst. From the start Stig Blomqvist was upholding the Saab reputation with some fast times but he was eventually to go out with a broken diff. Will Sparrow and Nigel Raeburn were proving that the Mini could still be competitive and the French Alpines were going well.

By the halfway point on Monday, the Rally was heading South through the Lake District and there were many gaps in the ranks. Some had simply gone off but many others had engine and transmission failures.

The Ford works team was out of the running. Only Clark remained and he was soon to retire with mechanical ailments. Tom Trana was already out, a victim of a broken flywheel and crankshaft.

The heavy Japanese Datsuns were also in trouble in the conditions and only one survived – in the experienced hands of Rauno Aaltonen.

Perhaps surprisingly, the Opel Dealer Team, from West Germany, and the durable but slow, Wartburg team from East Germany, were still plugging on and the Alpines too were going well. It looked as if Liz Crellin had the Ladies Prize sewn up and, most significantly, last year's winner, Harry Kallstrom, was moving steadily up the field.

But the Sputnik had his troubles. His Lancia had quite a bit of damage when it hit a bank at Llanwrda and only a transplant kept him going when the big end shells were transferred from team-mate Simo Lampinen's car after the latter's gearbox had failed.

The real drama had yet to come...

As a crowd gathered in the deepening dusk at the Centre Airport Hotel, many of them on the way home from work, no one knew for sure who would be the winner.

The last special stage was very, very close to the finish − at the military college of Camberley − and until the cars were through, the placings were uncertain.

Darkness fell and still the watchers waited patiently and quietly.

Kallstrom, living up to his nickname, was believed to be narrowly ahead of Jean-Luc Therier in one of the Alpines but with a number of stages close to the finish even the Results Team couldn't be absolutely sure due to the length of time the entire field took to go through any one stage.

Thus the general feeling amongst the watchers was that it all depended on who showed up at the Centre Airport − the distinctive-looking Lancia or the even more distinctive shape of the Alpine.

An Alpine did show through the gloom but it turned out to be the one driven by Andrew Cowan and Hamish Cardno. They were to be eventually placed fifth, the highest-placed British crew.

Then came dramatic news from Camberley, the final stage. The first cars to arrive had gone on to the stage which was a sea of mud. The conditions were so atrocious that it was decided to cancel the stage. But the cancellation had come too late for poor Therier for as his car floundered in the morass, a universal joint broke. The Frenchman was irretrievably stuck.

So Kallstrom scored a second successive victory for Lancia. Therier would undoubtedly have finished at least second and the fact that he did not do so cost the French team the European Constructors Championship which went instead to Porsche. The French took it in good part and were much more philosophical about it than many of us could have been.

It was a lucky break for the Germans because in second, third and fourth places came the Opel Kadett team, entered by Swedish dealers.

There was one good after-effect: the Camberley affair showed the organising committee that stages too close to the finish were nothing but a headache for all concerned.

'from Harrogate it started'...

1971 broke fresh ground with the Rally starting and finishing in the

Victory for the Sputnik in the 1970 Rally

Below *Makinen and Liddon hold aloft the Peall Trophy after winning the RAC in 1975. It was Makinen's hat-trick thus equalling Carlsson's record*

Colin Malkin surveying his 'works' Chrysler

Below *Consolation for the Frenchmen stuck on the Camberley stage – Lord Camden presents Jean-Luc Therier with an artist's impression of 'X marks the spot'*

Bjorn Waldegard and Hans Thorzelius, both RAC veterans, joined the Ford team in 1977

Below *Triumph TR7 engine bay, complete with 3500cc V8 engine*

Northern spa of Harrogate where hotels, police and local authorities had some experience of large scale motoring events, having played host for some years to the Mobil Economy Run.

In the third year of *Daily Mirror* sponsorship, the Rally went to Harrogate only after a strong bid by Bradford. The rivalry between the two places was fierce and led to several attempts at 'one upmanship', most of which were helpful to the publicity for the event.

It also contributed to the best rally film ever made – Barrie Hinchcliffe's 'from Harrogate it started'.

But for the moment, Bradford had to content itself with providing the most remarkable stage yet in an RAC – the sewerage works at Esholt.

Jack Kemsley tells a wonderful tale (probably apocryphal) of being conducted over the sewerage works by the Lord Mayor who pointed out that at one sharp bend a cluster of acid tanks lay in wait for the unwary. 'I'm a bit worried about that,' said the Lord Mayor, 'those tanks would dissolve a man and a car in about three minutes.' Said Jack, 'Yes, it's certainly a danger for the drivers – I can see what you're worried about.' 'Oh,' said the Lord Mayor, 'I'm not worried about the drivers but it would muck up Bradford's sewerage operation for a week.'

For the first and so far only time the start and finish was INDOORS. To be precise – in the Harrogate Exhibition Halls. It had many advantages, certainly for the spectators who were protected from the elements, but the *Mirror* felt that it detracted from the atmosphere of the event and so the idea was dropped after this one year.

With it went another idea which Jack Kemsley and the author evolved and still believe could be made worthwhile – a motor show and exhibition in one of the adjoining halls.

Castrol ran a cinema showing films designed to appeal to the enthusiast, several motor dealers had stands and there was a display of cars which had won or featured prominently in past rallies, amongst them Ian Appleyard's famous white Jaguar.

And it was Ian, a very successful motor agent in the North, who flagged the cars away from the start.

In the sequel, the event was dominated by the overseas entries. Not surprisingly, perhaps, since there were works teams from Lancia (winners for the past two years), Datsun, Saab, Skoda and the plodding but reliable Wartburgs.

The introduction of a number of stately home stages ('Mickey Mouse' stages, said many of the competitors) served their purpose in attracting many

Brian Culcheth and Johnstone Syer in the Team Unipart – Castrol Triumph Dolomite Sprint on the Bramham stage of the 1974 RAC

Roger Clark, 1976 RAC winner, on the road to victory in his Ford Escort RS 1800

spectators to areas where some degree of control could be exercised but they did not eliminate much of the field although on one a Mini failed to take a bend and went straight on to finish in the middle of an ornamental lake. The obvious surprise of the occupants made one of the most hilarious sequences in Barrie Hinchcliffe's film.

The Mini crew had to rescue themselves but at Esholt police frogmen were on hand either to rescue anyone unlucky enough to skid into the sewerage or to fish hopefully (only three minutes leeway, remember) for those even more unfortunate ones who dived into the acid!

But yet again it was the forests which sorted the men from the boys and saw a cluster of Finns and Swedes occupying the leading positions at the finish. In the end it proved a great comeback for Saab with Stig Blomqvist and Arne Hertz in first place and that consistent RAC performer, Carl Orrenius, third. Waldegard in a Porsche entered by himself split the Saabs. Lancia after two wins in a row could do no better than a sixth place for Lampinen and there was a glimmer of hope on the home front with Fords in fourth and fifth places, although their drivers were the redoubtable Finns, Makinen and Mikkola.

The prize-giving was an entertainment in itself. One nervous speaker kept flipping the microphone on-and-off: Jack Kemsley was given a 'This Is Your Life' presentation which had many of the audience fooled — they looked around for the TV cameras and Eamonn Andrews; and the Bradford Councillors pulled their master stroke. As the flashlights went off, they stood up bearing banners with slogans like 'Bradford for Wool', 'Bradford Is The Greatest' and so on.

Harrogate did its genteel best to ignore them...

Harrogate had certainly proved a success and no one questioned that the move from London had been a wise one. The Yorkshire crowds were enthusiastic and from the competitors point of view it was a great advantage having so much excellent rallying country so close to the start and finish. But with the cost of staging an international event growing apace it was essential to get some sort of deal from the town or city chosen as headquarters. Harrogate had been generous up to a point but charges for the exhibition halls, for example, had bitten into the budget; Bradford, although willing to bid high, was still awaiting the completion of extra hotel accommodation; and so it was York, with more than enough hotels and ready to make a realistic offer, who scooped the prize and for 1972 the Rally moved there. The Station Hotel was the HQ, the *Daily Mirror* was again the principal **180** sponsor and this time Unipart, the British Leyland spare parts subsidiary,

Rally at night....1

Rally at night....2

also contributed to the kitty, by the long arm of coincidence partly because Unipart's Dick Nelson and the author played cricket for Finchley many many years previously.

It was to be the start of a new era in the RAC, an era which was to see a British manufacturer triumphant, a pattern set for the rally for years to come and the emergence of an old supporter as a new main sponsor.

The RAC Rally swung into the mid-Seventies with renewed vigour...

Ford Triumphant

1972 MARKED the beginning of the most successful winning streak in history. Roger Clark and Tony Mason, driving a Ford Escort, became the first British drivers to win the event since 1959, and began a series of Ford victories which went on and on and on.

They took the lead at the end of the second of seventy special stages and stayed there to finish 3 minutes 25 seconds in front of the previous year's winner, Stig Blomqvist.

One man must have viewed Roger's victory with mixed feelings. Jim Porter, his regular co-driver, had given up the bucket seat beside Clark in order to become the full-time organiser of the event.

But Jim could take consolation from the wonderful job he did and continued to do in the difficult task of taking over from Jack Kemsley. Jack was not lost to the Rally but continued as Chairman of the Organising Committee.

If Harrogate had been a success, York was a jamboree. The Rally returned there in 1973 and for the second year Unipart supported the *Mirror* sponsorship.

And it moved a step nearer the big-time by becoming only the second sporting event after Test Match cricket to become the subject of a Post Office telephone results service.

The idea struck one morning whilst shaving (the usual and only time of day for any bright ideas to enter the Drackett cranium) and it was not with any feeling of confidence that the Post Office was approached.

Yet, once again, fortune was on our side.

The Post Office official responsible for developing this side of the Post *183*

Stig Blomqvist in his new RED SAAB 99 Turbo, ready for the 1979 RAC

Office's activities turned out to be an enthusiastic member of the Civil Service Motoring Association and a keen club rallyist.

Once he agreed to give the results service a trial, the overwhelming response of the rallying public made its continuance a certainty.

And for Ford, the rally itself was to be an even bigger triumph than the year before. With much of the drama in the five day, 2,000 mile epic coming in the final 169 miles on the Yorkshire Dales, the Saabs of Lampinen and Eklund and Bjorn Waldegard's BMW all came to grief in desperate bids to catch the leading Ford of Timo Makinen, who had been in front since the Saturday night.

So Fords sailed home 1-2-3.

Makinen and Henry Liddon shared the winning car, 1972 winner Roger Clark was second and the up-and-coming young Finn, Markku Alen was third.

Stuart Turner, Ford motor sport chief, could only say: 'This is beyond my wildest expectation.'

And for those who think rallying a frivolous pastime, it was estimated that this one had brought more than one million pounds in foreign currency into the country.

Lancia Stratos en route for the stratosphere in 1979

The final big change of the decade came before the 1974 Rally. IPC, who first through the *Daily Herald* and the *Sun*, and then through the *Daily Mirror*, had seen the event through so many difficult years, reluctantly decided to pull out, one of their reasons being the reluctance of television to give the Rally sponsor a fair break.

To the rescue came the merchant bank subsidiary of Natwest, Lombard, who for long had been associated in the business with the RAC and had given support in a modest way to the Rally almost since its inception as an International competition. As befitted financial wizards they came forward with realistic long-term proposals which safeguarded the event for years ahead and during those years Lombard's Chief Executive, Ron Barnes, and his henchmen Ken Warriner, Derek Darwent and Bob Evans, were to become familiar figures at Rally HQ.

The change in sponsor did not affect the venue for 1974. It was back to York, to the eager spectators at the York Race Course where the smell of chocolate-making mingled with the fog and the steam from the hot beef broth sold in the cause of charity by the York Lions Club, to the Edwardian distinction of the Royal Station Hotel and the more swinging but sometimes river-bound Viking, and to the first-class support given by the York Motor **185**

Club and the first-class hospitality by successive Lord Mayors.

The Rally itself brought about another Ford win but as the Duke of Wellington commented, 'It was a demned close run thing.' Fog decimated the field early on and it was the foreign teams which emerged intact, Datsun taking the honours from Fiat and Mazda.

However, Timo Makinen was again at his brilliant best and streaked home ahead of a mixed bag of Saabs, Lancias, Toyotas, Opels and Volvos.

And there was a glance back to yesteryear with Pat Moss-Carlsson winning the Ladies Award for Toyota.

This year a Clubman's event was held 'within' the main event and a Ford Escort (K. Thomas) won this too.

1975 was a duplicate year. York was again the venue and Makinen again the winner, a well-deserved hat-trick for one of the most popular drivers ever to set wheel in a British forest even although he was not as one newspaper described him, 'the well-known Scottish driver McKinnon'.

It was yet another sensational 1-2-3 for the Ford Escorts and for once Stuart Turner was speechless. Clark was again second behind Makinen and Tony Fowkes came in third ahead of another British driver, Tony Pond, in an Opel. In fact, it was one of the most encouraging results for British drivers as distinct from British cars for years.

The cars had been flagged away by Minister of Transport, Dr. John Gilbert, and afterwards he told Joan Drackett in an exclusive interview:

'I would like to congratulate the RAC and Lombard on the superb way in which they have organised this rally. They must be delighted both with the weather and the large crowds who have turned out to watch. It is particularly pleasing for those who have given up so much of their time in planning and organising this impressive demonstration. If only I had the time and talent, I would very much like to take part.'

If statistics mean anything, the figures subsequently published by Lombard were: 2 million spectators, 8.5 million television viewers, 100,000 column inches, 29 daily radio broadcasts and 8 TV newscasts, a 25 minute 'World of Sport' on TV, and 190,000 calls to the Post Office Results Service.

But it was time for another change...

Organisers and sponsors were agreed that to remain a true National as well as an International event, the Rally must move around the country and so for 1976, the ancient City of Bath, in the West Country, was chosen as venue.

Bath had a difficult row to hoe in following York and it is a measure of the City's success that everything ran quite smoothly and indeed 'off course'

Stately homes draw the crowds

THIS is the RAC Rally?

Start from Birmingham in 1978

many people commented that the prize presentation was the best in the history of the Rally.

And the first prize went once again to Ford, with Roger Clark taking the chequered flag for the second time and other Escorts driven by Waldegard and Billy Coleman in third and sixth places. Stig Blomqvist did well once again to finish second and it was largely due to him that the Saab team beat out Wartburg for the team prize. Again there was a Clubman's section and this was won by a Ford Escort (David Childs) — what else? Jill Robinson won the Ladies Award in — wait for it — a Ford Escort.

Despite the urgings of Bath's very attractive Lady Mayor, it was return to York in 1977, a return which ended in the sixth successive victory for Ford of Britain. This time Bjorn Waldegard was driving the winning car at the end of a five day 1900 miles event which included over 500 miles of special stages.

Of the 180 cars flagged away by Prince Michael of Kent, himself an enthusiastic rally driver, fewer than 70 survived for the York finish.

The start, for a change, had been from Wembley Stadium in London, which gave the South a glimpse of the Rally which had been rare in recent years.

End of the Rally....the author and Dean Delamont, former Director of Motor Sport for the RAC, relax over a drink....

Once away from North London, the weather was terrible and featured snow, sleet and torrential rain. The Escorts once more proved themselves all-purpose rally cars and only the valiant efforts of Hannu Mikkola (Toyota) prevented Fords filling the first five places. As it was, Brookes was third, Clark fourth, Dawson fifth and Hamalainen sixth. And Jill Robinson again took the Ladies Award. This time too there was no argument about the winning manufacturers team.

Stuart Turner and Peter Ashcroft can take a hint. Mikkola was in the Ford team for the 1978 Rally which centred for the first time on Birmingham. It has to be said that the heart of the motor industry was not the best place to run an international rally. The intimate atmosphere of places like York, Bath and Harrogate was lost and the City's tortuous one way system drove visitors to despair. One Finnish journalist commented: 'Heart of the motor car industry? There is nowhere you can drive a bloody car.'

The venue did not much worry Mikkola. He galloped home with a comfortable lead over his team-mates, Waldegard and Brookes for Ford's seventh straight win; the Escorts took the team award; more Escorts were first and second in the Private Entrants category; and Judy Simpson in another Escort won the Ladies.

It was no surprise when the announcement was made that the 1978 Lombard-RAC Rally would be held in Chester...

Which is where we came in.

End of the Rally....two helmets....and the rain

Appendix A

RESULTS OF RAC RALLY AND COACHWORK
COMPETITION 1932-1939

Note: In this period, the RAC Rally had only National Status and did not
become an International event until after the Second World War. The system
of awards was changed from time to time, hence the variations in the results
listed.

1932

Class 1 (over 1,100 cc)
1. Col. A.H. Loughborough   Lanchester 2,504 cc
2. J. Mercer   Daimler 4,018 cc
3. G.F. Dennison   Riley 1,633 cc
4. H.P. Henry   Armstrong-Siddeley 3,190 cc
5. Donald Healey   Invicta 4,467 cc
6. J.D. Siddeley   Armstrong-Siddeley 3,190 cc

Class 2 (under 1,100 cc)
1. V.E. Leverett   Riley 1,089 cc
2. Rupert St G. Riley   Riley 1,089 cc
3. G.H. Strong   Standard 1,005 cc
4. Mrs. M.M. Riley   Riley 1,089 cc
5. Mrs. Chris Staniland   Riley 1,089 cc
6. R.W. Petley   Riley 1,089 cc

Entries: 367   Starters: 341   Finishers: 312   *197*

Other awards

Ladies' prize
Class 1: Lady de Clifford (Lagonda)
Class 2: Mrs. M.M. Riley (Riley)

Team Prize

MCC 'D' Team:	Raymond Way (Rover)
	Donald Healey (Invicta)
	Col. A.H. Loughborough
	(Lanchester)

Coachwork Competition
The *Motor* Cup (for finest car over 1,100 cc, irrespective of class):
   J.E. Scott (Talbot '65')
The *Autocar* Cup (for finest car under 1,100 cc, irrespective of class):
   C.J. Joyce (Crossley Ten)

1933

Class 1 (over 16 hp)

1.	T.D.Wynn Weston	Rover 2,565 cc
2.	Donald Healey	Invicta 4,467 cc
3.	K. Hutchison	Ford 3,622 cc
4.	The Hon. Mrs. Chetwynd	Ford 3,622 cc
5.	H.E. Symons	Siddeley Special 4,960 cc
6.	Miss Fay Taylour	Ford 3,622 cc

Class 2 (over 10 hp and up to 16 hp)

1.	Miss Kitty Brunell	AC 1,991 cc
2.	C.M. Anthony	Aston Martin 1,493 cc
3.	M.C. Wilsk	Rover 1,577 cc
4.	C.F. Hurlock	AC 1,991 cc
5.	G.F. Searle	Rover 1,577 cc
6.	W.A.E. Hurlock	AC 1,991 cc

Class 3 (up to 10 hp)

| 1. | G. Dennison | Riley 1,089 cc |

2. F.R.G. Spikins	Singer 972 cc
3. F.C. Rolfe	Singer 972 cc
4. J. Hobbs	Riley 1,089 cc
5. V.E. Leverett	Riley 1,089 cc
6. Miss D.C.N. Champney	Riley 1,089 cc

Entries: 357   Starters: 340   Finishers: 308

Other awards

Ladies' Prize
Class 1: Hon. Mrs. Chetwynd (Ford)
Class 2: Miss Kitty Brunell (AC)
Class 3: Miss D.C.N. Champney (Riley)

Team Prize
Riley Motor Club 'B' Team: V.E. Leverett
                                 Rupert St G. Riley
                                 G. Dennison

Coachwork Competition
Champion car over 16 hp: C.W. Ward (Rolls-Royce)
Champion car, 10 hp to 16 hp: S.B. Wilks (Rover)
Champion car, up to 10 hp: C.J. Joyce (Crossley)

1934

Class 1 (over 16 hp)

1. T.D. Wynn-Weston	Rover 20 hp
2. H. Hillcoat	Ford V8 30 hp
3. Norman Black	Hudson Essex Terraplane 28 hp
4. J.E. Scott	Talbot 21 hp
5. J.B. Thompson	Ford V8 30 hp
6. E. Ainsworth	Avon Special 20 hp

Class 2 (over 10 hp and up to 16 hp)

1. S.B. Wilks	Rover 12 hp
2. F. Stanley Barnes	Singer 13 hp

199

3. C.F. Hurlock	AC Ace 16 hp
4. C.M. Anthony	Aston Martin 12 hp
5. H.W. Allingham	MG 12 hp
6. F. Stanley Barnes	Singer 13 hp

Class 3 (up to 10 hp)

1. F.R.G. Spikins	Singer 9 hp
2. J. Harrop	MG 8 hp
3. F. Stanley Barnes	Singer 9 hp
4. Victor Riley	Riley 9 hp
5. F.C. Rolfe	Singer 9 hp
6. Victor Riley	Riley 9 hp

Entries: 450   Starters: 384   Finishers: 351

Other awards

Ladies' Prize
Class 1: Miss R.M. Harker (Sunbeam)
Class 2: Mrs. K.E. Wilks (Rover)
Class 3: Miss J. Astbury (Singer)

Manufacturers' Team Prize

Singer 'B' Team:	W.J.B. Richardson
	A.H. Langley
	J.D. Barnes

Club Team Prize

Singer Motor Club:	A.C. Westwood
	W.M.D. Montgomery
	R.C. Tibbey

Coachwork Competition
Open cars: R.H. Gregory (Alvis)
Two-door closed cars: C.W. Ward (Bentley)
Four-door closed cars: W.M. Park (Rolls-Royce)

1935

There were no classifications this year. Finishers were awarded gold, silver or bronze awards. The gold, or first-class, went to competitors who lost no marks on arrival or inspection and subsequently did well in the eliminating tests. In the sequel, there were 106 gold awards. Drivers who qualified for those included Stanley Barnes, Sammy Davis, John Eason Gibson, Doreen Evans, Ray Gough, Alan Hess, Goff Imhof, Jack Kemsley, S.M. Lawry, Lord Waleran and Mrs. 'Bill' Wisdom.

Entries: 308   Starters: 281   Finishers: 241

Other awards

Coachwork Competition
Open cars: Captain C.C. Oxborrow (Vanden Plas Bentley)
Two-door closed cars: S.E. Sears (Salmons Bentley)
Four-door closed cars: W.M. Park (Park Ward Rolls-Royce)

1936

Group 1 (open cars up to 8 hp)
1. N.E. Bracey   MG

Group 2 (closed cars up to 8 hp)
1. C.E.A. Westcott   Austin Seven

Group 3 (open cars between 8 hp and 14 hp)
1. A.H. Langley   Singer

Group 4 (closed cars between 8 hp and 14 hp)
1. A.G. Imhof   Singer

Group 5 (open cars between 14 hp and 20 hp)
1. C.G. Pitt   Frazer-Nash-BMW

Group 6 (closed cars between 14 hp and 20 hp)
1. J.L. Finigan   Frazer-Nash-BMW

Group 7 (open cars over 20 hp)
1. F.R.G. Spikins   Spikins-Hudson-Special

Group 8 (closed cars over 20 hp)
1. S.E. Sears   Bentley

Entries: 316   Starters: 274   Finishers: 252

Other awards

Ladies' Prize (open cars)
1. Joan Richmond   Triumph

Ladies' Prize (closed cars)
1. M. Wilby   Armstrong-Siddeley

Manufacturers' Team Prize
1. Singer (F.S. Barnes, J.D. Barnes, A.H. Langley)
2. Singer (M.H. Lawson, W.J.B. Richardson, A.G. Imhof)

Club Team Prize
1. Singer Motor Club (Midland Centre) (F.S. Barnes, J.D. Barnes,
    A.H. Langley)
2. Singer Motor Car Club (Northern Centre) (W.C. Butler, G.N. Frame Jnr.,
    H.E. Bradley)

Coachwork Competition
Open Cars
1. J.L. Sears   Alvis O.F.-Vanden Plas
Two-door Closed Cars
1. Charles Follett   Alvis Follett-Vanden Plas
Four-door Closed Cars
1. Col. R. Rippon   Humber Rippon Bros

1937

Group 1 (open cars up to 10 hp)
1. H.F.S. Morgan   Morgan

Group 2 (closed cars up to 10 hp)
1. B.W. Fursdon   Wolseley

Group 3 (open cars up to 15 hp)
1. J.F.A. Clough   Riley

Group 4 (closed cars up to 15 hp)
1. A.L. Pearce   Triumph

Group 5 (open cars over 15 hp)
1. J. Harrop   SS

Group 6 (closed cars over 15 hp)
1. D. Impanni   Frazer-Nash-BMW

Entries: 213   Starters: 192   Finishers: 184

Other awards

Ladies' Prize (open cars)
1. The Viscountess Chetwynd   Ford

Ladies' Prize (closed cars)
1. S.D. Bradley   Triumph

Manufacturers' Team Prize
1. SS Cars Ltd (T.H. Wisdom, Hon. Brian Lewis, E.W. Rankin)
2. Singer Motors Ltd (F.S. Barnes, J.D. Barnes, A.H. Langley)

Club Team Prize
1. Singer Motor Car Club A Team (F.S. Barnes, J.D. Barnes, A.H. Langley)
2. Yorkshire Sports Car Club B Team (E.A. Denny, T.C. Wise,
    J. Kingston-Whittaker)

Coachwork Competition
Open cars
1. L.G.O. Prideaux-Brune   Aston Martin
Two-door Closed Cars
1. R.L. Walkerley   MG Salmons   *203*

Four-door Closed Cars
1. C.F.G. Barraclough   Daimler Charlesworth

Although an overall classification for the Rally did not become standard practice until many years later, an unofficial standing, compiled at the time of the 1937 event, may interest the reader:

1. J. Harrop	SS Jaguar	943 marks
2. T.H. Wisdom	SS Jaguar	940.2
3. J. Flint	Frazer-Nash-BMW	939.4
4. E.H. Jacob	SS Jaguar	938.2
5. Hon. Brian Lewis	SS Jaguar	
6. J.F.A. Clough	Riley	937.4

1938

Group 1 (open cars up to 10 hp)
1. G.H. Goodall   Morgan

Group 2 (closed cars up to 10 hp)
1. B.W. Fursdon   Wolseley

Group 3 (open cars between 10 hp and 15 hp)
1. C.M. Anthony   Aston Martin

Group 4 (closed cars between 10 hp and 15 hp)
1. A.L. Pearce   Triumph

Group 5 (open cars over 15 hp)
1. J. Harrop   SS

Group 6 (closed cars over 15 hp)
1. D. Loader   Ford

Entries: 255   Starters: 237   Finishers: 231

Ladies' Prize (open cars)
1. Mrs. K. Hague   Riley

Ladies' Prize (closed cars)
1. O. Bailey   Rover

Manufacturers' Team Prize
1. Riley (Auty & Lees Ltd) (J.F.A. Clough, G.H. Beetson, Mrs. K. Hague)
2. Ford (Beecholme Motors) (W.C.N. Norton, H. Koppenhagen, D. Loader)

Club Team Prize
1. Junior Car Club C (W.C.N. Norton, H. Koppenhagen, D. Loader)
2. Lancashire A.C. A (J.F.A. Clough, C.E. Stothert, H.E. Bradley)

Coachwork Competition
Four-door closed cars
1. Col. R. Rippon   Daimler Straight Eight
Two-door closed cars
1. J. Barclay   Bentley 30 hp
Open cars
1. D. Healey   Triumph 14 hp
Drop-head Coupes
1. Lord Waleran   Lagonda 42 hp

For the second successive year, J. Harrop (SS Jaguar) would have been placed first had there been an official overall classification.

1939

Group 1
1. G.H. Goodall   Morgan

Group 2
1. H.F.S. Morgan   Morgan

Group 3
1. M.H. Lawson   HRG

Group 4
1. G.S. Davison   Triumph

Group 5
1. A.F.P. Fane   Frazer-Nash-BMW

Group 6
1. H.J. Aldington   Frazer-Nash-BMW

Entries: 224   Starters: 200   Finishers: 192

Other awards

Ladies' Prize (open cars)
1. Mrs. K. Hague   Riley 12

Ladies' Prize (closed cars)
1. Viscountess Chetwynd   Ford V8 30

Manufacturers' Team Prize
1. Frazer-Nash-BMW (L.G. Johnson, D.H. Murray, A.F.P. Fane)
2. HRG (A.E.S. Curtis, M.H. Lawson, G.H. Robins)

Club Team Prize
1. Junior Car Club (L.G. Johnson, D.H. Murray, A.F.P. Fane)
2. SS Car Club (A.D.C. Gordon, C.J. Gibson, C. Mann)

Coachwork Competition
Open cars
1. Miss D.M. Stanley-Turner   Alvis
Two-door closed cars
1. A.L. Goodrich   Talbot Ten
Four-door closed cars
1. J. Barclay   Rolls-Royce
Drop-head Coupes
1. N.A. Bronsten   Bentley

Unofficial overall 'winner' of the Rally was A.F.P. Fane (Frazer-Nash-BMW) who retained 916.4 marks out of 1,000.

Appendix B

RESULTS OF RAC INTERNATIONAL RALLY
OF GREAT BRITAIN 1951 ONWARDS

1951

There was no General Category and so no overall winner, the entry being divided into four classes.

Open cars up to 1,500 cc

1. J.V.S. Brown	HRG	120.57
2. Mrs. Nancy Mitchell	HRG	120.61
3. R.H. Hopkinson	MG	121.53
4. Marcel Becquart	Jowett Jupiter	122.06

Closed cars up to 1,500 cc

1. J. Reading	MG	124.40
2. J. Van der Mark	Jowett Javelin	126.63
3. J.L. Shaw	MG	127.75
4. S. Ginn	Jowett Javelin	129.92

Open cars over 1,500 cc

1. Ian Appleyard	Jaguar XK120	109.61
2. P.H.G. Morgan	Morgan	112.99
3. W.A.G. Goodall	Morgan	114.55
4. Don Bennett	Jaguar XK120	116.30

Closed cars over 1,500 cc

1. R. Harper	Vauxhall	125.03
2. G.R. Hartwell	Sunbeam-Talbot	126.21
3. W.K. Elliott	Bristol	126.76
4. L.F. Parham	Bristol	128.23

Entries: 267   Starters: 229   Finishers: 185

Other awards

Ladies' Prize (open cars)

1. M. Newton	Jaguar XK120	120.51

Ladies' Prize (closed cars)

1. Sheila Van Damm Mrs. 'Bill' Wisdom	Hillman Minx	145.68

Team Prize
1. Morgan (W.A.G. Goodall, P.H.G. Morgan, W.S. Steel)

Note: Although there was no overall winner, the best performance of the Rally was that of Ian and Pat Appleyard (Jaguar XK120) who lost only 109.61 marks.

1952

Open cars, unlimited

1. 'Goff' Imhof	Allard-Cadillac	183.80
2. C. Broadhead	Jaguar XK120	185.00
3. Ian Appleyard	Jaguar XK120	186.60
4. B.D. Christie	Jaguar XK120	190.80
5. B. Reece	Morgan	198.20
6. H.G. Morgan	Morgan	199.40

Closed cars, 2$^{1/2}$-litre

1. Marcel Becquart	Jowett	222.60
2. R.P. Lane	Riley	227.00
3. A.P. Warren	Riley	230.40

4. L.F. Parham	Bristol	236.40
5. J.A. Smith	Ford	239.40
6. G.S. Prout	Austin	241.00

Closed cars, unlimited

1. W.S. White	Ford	240.40
2. A. Park	Allard	243.00
3. G. Smith	Jaguar	243.80
4. A. Stewart	Bentley	245.80
5. P. Keay	Jaguar	248.80
6. G. Shanely	Austin	252.20

Entries: 231   Starters: 242   Finishers: 199

Other awards

Ladies' Prize (open cars)
1. M. Newton   Jaguar XK120

Ladies' Prize (closed cars)
1. C. Sadler   Rover

Team Prize
1. Morgan (P.H.G. Morgan, W.A.G. Goodall, W.S. Steel)

Note: Although there was again no General Category, the outstanding performances for both open and closed cars were officially recognised this year. 'Goff' Imhof accordingly won the award for open cars and Marcel Becquart that for the closed. Imhof's performance was, of course, the best of the Rally.

1953

General Category

1. Ian Appleyard	Jaguar XK120	343.44 & 29.37*
2. Ronnie Adams	Sunbeam-Talbot	394.90 & 22.77
3. 'Goff' Imhof	Allard-Cadillac	353.30 & 19.51
4. J.C. Broadhead	Jaguar XK120	355.84 & 16.97 *209*

5. Air Vice-Marshal Don Bennett	Jaguar XK120	16.31
6. J.L. Shaw	MG Saloon	12.45

Entries: 205   Starters: 194   Finishers: 154

Other awards

Best performance — sports cars
1. Ian Appleyard   Jaguar XK120

Best performance — touring cars
1. Ronnie Adams   Sunbeam-Talbot

Ladies' Award
1. Sheila Van Damm   Sunbeam Talbot

Team Prize
1. Jaguar (Ian Appleyard, W.C.N. Grant Norton and Frank Grounds)

*Note: As can be seen, a general category governed the Rally this year, the final order being decided on a figure of merit based on 11 tests (second column above). The first column is for road marks lost.

1954

1. Johnny Wallwork	Triumph	416.67
2. Peter Cooper	Triumph	435.05
3. Cuth Harrison	Ford Zephyr	440.50
4. Peter Harper	Sunbeam-Talbot	441.00
5. W.D. Bleakley	Triumph	445.85
6. Ronnie Adams	Alvis	449.70

Entries: 239   Starters: 229   Finishers: 164

Other awards

Ladies' Prize
1. M. Walker   Triumph   492.25

Best performance – touring class
1. Cuth Harrison   Ford Zephyr   440.50

Team Prize
1. Ford No. 2 (Cuth Harrison, J.G. Reece, and Mrs Nancy Mitchell)
2. Triumph No. 2 (B. Dickson, D. Done, Miss M. Walker)

1955

1. Jimmy Ray	Standard Ten	258.10
2. H.E. Rumsey	Triumph TR2	462.30
3. W.K. Richardson	Standard Ten	559.50
4. Ronnie Adams	Alvis	583.40

Entries: 240   Starters: 238   Finishers: 168

Other awards

Ladies' Prize
1. Sheila Van Damm   Sunbeam   1,603.20

Team Prize
1. Standard (Jimmy Ray, J.H.B. Dickson, W.K. Richardson)

1956

1. Lyndon Sims	Aston Martin	29.20
2. Ian Appleyard	Jaguar	50.00
3. Dr J.T. Spare	Morgan	54.80
4. W.D. Bleakley	Jaguar	65.10
5. Peter Cooper	Standard Ten	81.60
6. Douglas Johns	Austin	82.90

Other awards

Ladies' Prize
1. A. Palfrey	Austin	419.10

Team Prize
1. Austin (Mrs Johns, Gerry Burgess and Jack Sears)

1957

The Suez Crisis, and the subsequent introduction of petrol rationing led to the abandonment of the 1957 event.

1958

1. Peter Harper	Sunbeam	657.00
2. R.A. Goldburn	Standard Pennant	1,179.30
3. Tommy Gold	Standard Pennant	1,231.40
4. Pat Moss	Morris Minor 1000	1,474.50
5. W.H. Wadham	Morris Minor 1000	1,507.30
6. C. Corbishley	Standard Ten	1,919.15

Entries: 205   Starters: 196   Finishers: 130

Other awards

Ladies' Prize
1. Pat Moss	Morris Minor 1000	1,474.50

Manufacturers' Team Prize
1. Standard No. 1 (R.A. Goldbourn, T. Gold and C. Corbishley)

Club Team Prize
No award

1959

1. Gerry Burgess	Ford Zephyr	33
2. Tommy Gold	Austin-Healey Sprite	42
3. Mike Sutcliffe	Riley 1.5	43
4. Donald Morley	Austin-Healey	44
5. E. Malkin	Sunbeam Rapier	46
6. P.H.G. Morgan	Morgan Plus Four	48

Entries: 139   Starters: 131   Finishers: 53

Other awards

Ladies' Prize
1. Anne Hall   Ford Anglia   309

Manufacturers' Team Prize
1. Standard-Triumph No. 2 (Annie Soisbault, E. Hodson and David Siegle-Morris)
2. Standard-Triumph No. 1 (Keith Ballisat, Tiny Lewis and Peter Bolton)

Club Team Prize
1. BRDC (Cuth Harrison, Peter Jopp and Sydney Allard)
2. Folkestone and East Kent Car Club (M.J. Gethring, H.J. Richmond, John La Trobe, J.H. Spiers)

1960

1. Erik Carlsson	Saab	0
2. John Sprinzel	Sebring Sprite	2
3. Donald Morley	Austin-Healey 3000	2
4. Jack Sears	Jaguar 3.8	3
5. Johnny Wallwork	Volvo	3
6. David Siegle-Morris	Morris	3

Entries: 180   Starters: 172   Finishers: 138   *213*

Other awards

Ladies' Prize
1. Anne Hall   Ford Anglia   5

Manufacturers' Team Prize
1. BMC (Donald Morley, Pete Riley and J. Williamson)
2. Ford (G.K. Armstrong, A. Pitts and G.P. Crabtree)

Club Team Prize
1. London M.C. 'A' (J.N. Easten, Bill Bengry and Erik Carlsson)
2. W. Essex C.C. (Ken Chambers, R.N. Richards and C. Bent-Marshall)

1961

1. Erik Carlsson	Saab	89
2. Pat Moss	Austin-Healey 3000	129
3. Peter Harper	Sunbeam	150
4. Paddy Hopkirk	Sunbeam	166
5. David Siegle-Morris	Austin-Healey	170
6. Gunnar Andersson	Volvo	184

Entries: 161   Starters: 150   Finishers: 81

Other awards

Ladies' Prize
1. Pat Moss   Austin-Healey 3000   129

Manufacturers' Team Prize
1. Sunbeam-Talbot (Peter Harper, Paddy Hopkirk and Peter Procter)
2. MG (Tommy Gold, Mike Sutcliffe and D. Astle)

Club Team Prize
1. Falkirk & District M.C. (Logan Morrison, R.S. Skelly and Tommy Paton)
2. Volkswagen Owners Club (Bill Bengry, R. McElminney and
J.R. McSpadden)

1962

1. Erik Carlsson	Saab	204
2. Paddy Hopkirk	Austin-Healey 3000	264
3. Pat Moss	Austin-Healey 3000	314
4. Tiny Lewis	Sunbeam Rapier	349
5. Rauno Aaltonen	Morris Mini-Cooper	352
6. Henry Taylor	Ford Anglia	354

Entries: 165   Starters: 157   Finishers: 102

Other awards

Ladies' Prize
1. Pat Moss	Austin-Healey 3000	314

Manufacturers' Team Prize
1. BMC (Rauno Aaltonen, Logan Morrison and Timo Makinen)
2. Standard-Triumph (J.J. Thuner, John Sprinzel and Mike Sutcliffe)

Club Team Prize
1. Knowledale 1 (Erik Carlsson, F. Crossley and Tommy Paton)
2. Maidstone & Mid-Kent (J.W. Spiers, M. Day and C. Elsewood)

1963

1. Tom Trana	Volvo	246
2. Harry Kallstrom	Volkswagen	293
3. Erik Carlsson	Saab	293
4. Paddy Hopkirk	Morris Cooper S	306
5. Timo Makinen	Austin-Healey 3000	311
6. Henry Taylor	Ford Cortina	347

Entries: 171   Starters: 163   Finishers: 91

Other awards

Ladies' Prize
1. Pat Moss   Ford Cortina

Manufacturers' Team Prize
1. Ford (Pat Moss, Pete Riley and Henry Taylor)
2. Volkswagen (B. Jansson, Bengt Soderstrom and Harry Kallstrom)

Club Team Prize
1. Chelmsford M.C. (R. Richards, A.T. Lobb, E.J. Hatchett)
2. Airedaile & Pennine C.C. (B.M. Chippindale, C.G. Wood, J.C. Tordoff)

1964

1. Tom Trana	Volvo	3510
2. Timo Makinen	Austin-Healey 3000	4631
3. Vic Elford	Ford	4860
4. Pat Moss	Saab	5006
5. Bengt Soderstrom	Ford	5113
6. Roy Fidler	Triumph	5292

Entries: 180   Starters: 158   Finishers: 89

Other awards

Ladies' Prize
1. Pat Moss   Saab

Manufacturers' Team Prize
1. Ford (Vic Elford, David Siegle-Morris and Henry Taylor)
No other team finished.

Club Team Prize
1. Alan Frazer Racing Team (John La Trobe, Bill Bengry and Adrian Boyd)
2. Sevenoaks & District Motor Club (D.H. Ray, P.W. Ward and

B.I. Stevens)

1965

1. Rauno Aaltonen	BMC Cooper S	531.23
2. Timo Makinen	Austin-Healey	534.31
3. Jerry Larsson	Saab Sport	537.18
4. Erik Carlsson	Saab Sport	540.33
5. Roy Fidler	Triumph 2000	554.16
6. J. Lusenius	BMC Cooper S	560.28

Entries: 168   Starters: 163   Finishers: 62

Other awards

Ladies' Prize
1. Pat Moss   Saab Sport   577.27

Manufacturers' Team Prize
1. Rootes (Rosemary Smith, Andrew Cowan and Tiny Lewis)
2. Wartburg (K. Rodiger, K. Otto and G. Ruttinger)

Club Team Prize
No award

1966

1. Bengt Soderstrom	Ford Lotus Cortina	475.15
2. Harry Kallstrom	BMC Cooper S	488.50
3. Tom Trana	Volvo	489.50
4. Rauno Aaltonen	BMC Cooper S	490.22
5. Tony Fall	BMC Cooper S	495.17
6. Lars Damberg	Renault 1300	496.34

Entries: 147   Starters: 144   Finishers: 63

Other awards

Ladies' Prize
1. Pat Moss   Saab Sport   503.12

Manufacturers' Team Prize
No award

Club Team Prize
1. Rhyl & District (M. Esmor-Thomas, B. Williams and W.B. Jones)
2. Northern Rally Competitors (P. Gelder, F. Davies and M.J. Telford)

1967

Rally cancelled owing to national outbreak of foot-and-mouth disease.

1968

1. Simo Lampinen	Saab V4	650.34
2. Carl Orrenius	Saab V4	666.04
3. Jim Bullough	Ford Escort	715.08
4. Phil Cooper	BMC Cooper S	731.45
5. B.J. Wilkinson	Ford Escort	747.29
6. John Barnes	Peugot 204	759.33

Entries: 114   Starters: 96   Finishers: 32

Other awards

Ladies' Prize
No award

Manufacturers' Team Prize
No award

Club Team Prize
218   No award

European Club Rally (run in conjunction with RAC)

1. Rod Cooper	Ford Lotus Cortina	685.23
2. Bob Bean	Ford Cortina	702.44
3. N.F. Cook	Ford Anglia	848.41

Entries: 16   Starters: 16   Finishers: 3

1969

1. Harry Kallstrom	Lancia	479.17
2. Carl Orrenius	Saab	483.32
3. Tony Fall	Lancia	494.36
4. Ove Andersson	Ford	494.46
5. Haken Lindberg	Saab	495.32
6. Roger Clark	Ford	497.04

Entries: 158   Starters: 151   Finishers: 69

Other awards

Ladies' Prize
1. Jill Robinson   BMW   691.54

Manufacturers' Team Prize
1. Nissan-Datsun (Rauno Aaltonen, J.L. Simonian and John Sprinzel)
2. BLMC (Triumph) (Andrew Cowan, Paddy Hopkirk and Brian Culcheth)

Club Team Prize
No award

1970

1. Harry Kallstrom	Lancia	541.50
2. Ove Erikson	Opel	544.18
3. Lille-Bror Nasenius	Opel	553.18

4. Jan Henriksson	Opel	556.08
5. Andrew Cowan	Alpine	560.20
6. Gerard Larousse	Porsche	561.04

Entries: 205   Starters: 196   Finishers: 67

Other awards

Ladies' Prize
1. Elizabeth Crellin   Austin Cooper   684.33

Manufacturers' Team Prize
1. Opel (O. Erikson, L. Nasenius and J. Henriksson)
2. V.E.B.A.E. (Hommel, Gries, Cylmbacher)

Club Team Prize
1. Sutton & Cheam (Fowkes, Thurlow, Wareing)
2. CSMA (Cook, Siemssen, Finch)

1971

1. Stig Blomqvist	Saab	450.47
2. Bjorn Waldegard	Porsche	454.00
3. Carl Orrenius	Saab	460.01
4. Hannu Mikkola	Ford	460.05
5. Timo Makinen	Ford	461.00
6. Simo Lampinen	Lancia	465.16

Entries: 250   Starters: 231   Finishers: 104

Other awards

Ladies' Prize
1. Marie Claude Beaumont   Opel   529.59

Manufacturers' Team Prize
1. Saab (S. Blomqvist, P. Eklund, C. Orrenius)
220 2. Ford (Clark, Mikkola, Makinen)

Club Team Prize
1. Brent (Childs, J. Williams, Harris)
2. Port Talbot MC (Bynon, Jenkins, Perens)
3. Middx County AC (Chamberlain, Lestrange, Slaughter)

1972

1. Roger Clark	Ford	410.07
2. Stig Blomqvist	Saab	413.32
3. Anders Kullang	Opel	419.57
4. Harry Kallstrom	Lancia	421.38
5. Simo Lampinen	Lancia	422.30
6. Ove Eriksson	Opel	424.53

Entries: 200   Starters: 191   Finishers: 80

Other Awards

Ladies' Prize
1. Marie Claude Beaumont   Opel   477.45

Manufacturers' Team Prize
1. Opel (A. Kullang, O. Eriksson, L.B. Nasenius)
2. Datsun (Aaltonen, Fall, Fidler)

Club Team Prize
No award

1973

1. Timo Makinen	Ford	407.08
2. Roger Clark	Ford	412.23
3. Marku Alen	Ford	415.26
4. Per-Inge Wolfridsson	Volvo	421.13
5. J-P Nicholas	Alpine Renault	423.08
6. Gunnar Blomqvist	Opel	425.44

Entries: 241 (including Clubman)
Starters: 198 International
               38 Clubman
Finishers: 91 International
               24 Clubman

Other Awards

Ladies' Prize

1. Eeva Heinonen	Volvo	468.58

Manufacturers
No Award

Club Team
Shipley & District MC

Trade
Crystal RalleSport-Hull

Clubmans Rally

1.	B. Evans	Porsche Carrera	269.33
2.	F. Henderson	Ford Escort	272.36
3.	M. Dale	Ford Capri	273.28
4.	P. Rook	Ford Cortina	273.47
5.	J. Rhodes	Ford Escort	276.38
6.	R. Beeby	Ford Escort	278.24

1974

1.	Timo Makinen	Ford Escort	482.39
2.	Stig Blomqvist	Saab	484.19
3.	Sandro Munari	Lancia Stratos	491.55
4.	Bjorn Waldegaard	Toyota	493.54
5.	Walter Roehrl	Opel	495.52
6.	Per Inge Walfridsson	Volvo	496.06

Entries: 250 (including Clubman)
Starters: 190 International
           44 Clubman
Finishers: 83 International
           20 Clubman

Other awards

Ladies' Prize

1. Pat Moss-Carlsson	Toyota	545.56

Manufacturers

1. Datsun Dealers Team	1535.29
2. Fiat Team	1545.47
3. Mazda G.B.	1788.18

Club Team

1. Tynemouth-District M.C.	1734.44
2. Civil Service Motoring Assoc.	1863.45

Clubmans Rally

1. K. Thomas	Ford Escort	326.34
2. C. Daisy	Avenger	328.03
3. J. Coxon	Mini Cooper	332.03
4. W. Rose	Ford Escort	332.35
5. D. Barker	Ford Escort	336.46
6. J. Harmer	BLMC Cooper	340.54

1975

1. Timo Makinen	Ford Escort	360.44
2. Roger Clark	Ford Escort	361.57
3. Tony Fowkes	Ford Escort	366.11
4. Tony Pond	Opel Kadett	372.26
5. Erik Aaby	Ford Escort	374.14
6. Billy Coleman	Ford Escort	376.38

Entries: 250	Starters: 236	Finishers: 104

Other Awards

Ladies' Prize
Trine Jensen	Ford Escort	458.03

Manufacturers
Dealer Team Vauxhall	1182.24
Skoda	1214.08

Club Team
BTRDA 'B'	1335.32
Knowldale C.C.	1450.27

Trade
No Award

1976

1. Roger Clark	Ford Escort	362.26
2. Stig Blomqvist	Saab 99	367.03
3. Bjorn Waldegaard	Ford Escort	367.55
4. Sandra Munari	Lancia Stratos	368.49
5. Ove Andersson	Toyota Corolla	371.43
6. Billy Coleman	Ford Escort	371.48

Entries:	257 (Int. & Clubmans)
Starters:	200 (International)
	39 (Clubmans)
Finishers:	71 (International)
	21 (Clubmans)

Other Awards

Ladies' Prize
Jill Robinson	Ford Escort	430.41

Manufacturers
1. Saab	1309.45
2. Wartburg	1423.37

Club

1. Lincolnshire-Louth M.C.		1423.37

Clubmans Rally

1. David Childs	Ford Escort	236.02
2. J. Williams	Ford Escort	237.29
3. Gordon Jarvis	Rapier H120	241.32
4. Alan Patis	Ford Escort	245.09
5. S. Webster	Vauxhall Magnum	246.46
6. Tony Trotman	Marina	251.40

1977

1. Bjorn Waldegaard	Ford Escort	501.26
2. Hannu Mikkola	Toyota Celica	503.49
3. Russell Brookes	Ford Escort	511.55
4. Roger Clark	Ford Escort	516.21
5. Andy Dawson	Ford Escort	519.46
6. Kyosti Hamamlainen	Ford Escort	522.17

Entries: 250 (International & Clubmans)
Starters: 180 International
            28 Clubman
Finishers: 67 International
            12 Clubman

Other Awards

Ladies' Prize

1. Jill Robinson	Ford Escort	639.51

Manufacturers
1. Ford
2. Skoda

Club Team
No Award

Clubmans Rally

1. David Thompson	Vauxhall Firenza	287.07
2. John Thompson	Ford Mexico	305.10
3. Mike May	Ford Escort	311.04
4. Nicky Porter	Mercedes	318.40
5. John Banks	Ford Escort	319.11
6. Ed Davies	Ford Escort	320.23

1978

1. Hannu Mikkola	Ford Escort	527.23
2. Bjorn Waldegaard	Ford Escort	532.41
3. Russell Brookes	Ford Escort	538.55
4. Tony Pond	TR7 V8	543.09
5. Anders Kullang	Opel Kadett GTE	553.48
6. Walter Rohrl	Fiat Abarth	557.47

Entries: 200   Starters: 168   Finishers: 61

Other Awards

Manufacturers' Award
1. Ford Motor Company		1598.59
2. Rallye Team Wartburg		2156.27

Private Entrants
1. Charles Samson	Ford Escort	594.02
2. Alan Carter	Ford Escort	611.14

Ladies' Award
1. Judy Simpson	Ford Escort	820.49

1979

1. Hannu Mikkola   Ford Escort   483.38

2. Russell Brookes	Ford Escort	494.07
3. Timo Salonen	Datsun	496.22
4. Ari Vatanen	Ford Escort	499.53
5. Markku Alen	Lancia Stratos	500.23
6. John Taylor	Ford Escort	504.01

Entries: 224   Starters: 175   Finishers: 74

Other Awards

Ladies' Award
   Marja-Liisa Korpi   Ford Escort   600.52

Manufacturers' Team
Ford Motor Co. Ltd. (Mikkola, Brookes, Vatanen)

Index